Cinderella Doesn't Live Here Anymore

How to Manifest ALL You Desire to Live Happily Ever After

Published by
MavenMark Books (an imprint of HenschelHaus Publishing, Inc.)
2625 South Greely Street, Suite 201
Milwaukee, WI 53207
www.HenschelHausBooks.com
Tel: 608-576-9747
Fax: 262-565-2058
Please contact the publisher for quantity discounts and permissions.

ISBN: 978-1-59598-098-4
LCCN: 2010928131

Design by: Lindsey Abendschein
Cover design by: Lindsey Abendschein

Printed in the United States of America.

Cinderella Doesn't Live Here Anymore

How to Manifest ALL You Desire to Live Happily Ever After

Nancy Retzlaff

MAVEN
MARK
BOOKS

Table of Contents

Dedication .... page *i*

Grateful Acknowledgements .... page *ii*

Part I: Beyond Illusion Lies Divinity .... page 1

    Chapter 1: Wishful Thinking .... page 2

    Chapter 2: The Bowl of Truth .... page 11

        Consciousness and Energy .... page 16

        I, Too, Had a Dream .... page 18

Part II: How to Get Rid of the Heebie-Jeebies .... page 21

    Chapter 3: Releasing Fear .... page 22

        Comparisons: The Ticket to Hell .... page 23

        A Principle of Aikido .... page 27

        Triumph over Terror .... page 31

        Know Thyself .... page 34

        To Become Quiet and Peaceful: Breathe .... page 41

        Exercise .... page 49

        The Great Shakedown .... page 50

        How to Meditate .... page 52

        Meditation Exercise .... page 54

    Chapter 4: If You Can Conceive It, You Can Achieve It .... page 58

        Affirmation and Visualization .... page 58

        How to Kick a Habit .... page 60

        Affirmation and Visualization Exercise .... page 70

        Putting Visualization to Work .... page 70

        Creating a New Reality .... page 72

Exercises   page   75

Only on Sunday   page   75

Exercises   page   76

Second Exercise   page   77

Chapter 5: The Greatest Problem Becomes
the Greatest Gift   page   78

You Can't Heal What You Don't Feel   page   78

Summary   page   79

Part III: From Fear into Mastery   page   81

Chapter 6: Forgiveness: The Greatest of All Miracles   page   82

Forgiveness Exercise   page   85

More Methods to Release Emotions   page   89

Chapter 7: Mirror, Mirror on the Wall   page   95

Chapter 8: Two Men Named Dick   page 102

Part IV: Happily Ever After   page 111

Chapter 9: The Joy of Relationships   page 112

Fun with Relationships   page 114

Shadow Boxing   page 116

The Power of Healing   page 116

The Great Debate   page 119

The Law of Attraction   page 122

The Great Marriage   page 123

Words to Live By   page 124

Chapter 10: The Power of Surrender   page 126
    Babaji   page 129
    Prosperity Reigns   page 130
Chapter 11: The Divine Comedy   page 136
    The Circle of Women   page 136
    Sun Bear   page 138
    The Call of the Dolphins   page 141
    You Are the Master of Your Destiny   page 144
    Maybe It's All Just a Dream   page 145
    Death: The Greatest Illusion of Them All   page 146
    The Great Symphony   page 147
    I Am That I AM   page 148
    I Am   page 149
    Aloha: To Love Is to Be Happy With   page 150
    U.S. Airways   page 151
    Prepare for Lift Off!   page 152
    Saved by the Plow   page 152
    The Whale of a Tale   page 153
    Summary   page 155
    A Diamond   page 156
    People Who Dream   page 157

Dedication

This book is lovingly dedicated to my beloved husband, Ray, who continually teaches me who I am, to our children who patiently made me grow up, to my brother-in-law Dick, my brother John, and to all those beautiful women out there who often work diligently in thankless jobs to make the world a better place.

This is your time. The feminine energy is now emerging to take its rightful place in partnership with the masculine. It brings with it love, justice, gentleness, and peace to create Heaven on Earth. May you join your light with it, transform the world, and be Joyous!

Grateful Acknowledgements

I am so grateful to my editor, Carolyn Kott Washburne, and to Larry Peterson, Deidre Heppell, and Alex Olson, whose tireless hours at the computer have saved this book from that place in the fifth dimension where the computer sends words into obscurity, and to my beloved friends who have supported me through this project: Lynne Austin, Annette Dillon, Patti Genko, Nate Hall, Glen Jeansonne, Mary Ann Morrissey, Carol Roberts, Susan Rockhill, Sherry Rudrud, and Anne Smith.

My deep gratitude also goes to my teachers, Babaji, Ramtha, and Noel Street, whose guidance continues to inspire me to reach onward and upward.

Thanks also to Kira Henschel, whose friendship, love, and faith in me has brought this book into reality.

Part I

Beyond Illusion
Lies Divinity

chapter 1

Wishful Thinking

In their search for love, peace, joy, and security in their lives, women are often looking in all the wrong places. They look outside themselves to someone or something else, rather than within, which guarantees that they will never find it. Cinderella was the dream of little girls everywhere for years and years. In the 1950s, it was expected that they would all meet "Mr. Right," get married, and live happily ever after, just like in the fairy tale. He would give her all she would ever need, and make her gloriously happy for the rest of her life. That hardly ever happened. Often the prince turned back into the toad, and they both lived unhappily ever after.

Even today, people search starry-eyed for their soul mates or a warm port in the storm. They question psychics and astrologers for the answer to when Prince Charming will arrive. Some men also are on the lookout for Princess Perfect to take care of them forever. This is akin to winning the lottery, where all your problems would be over forever. That rarely happens, either.

Cinderella embodies the concept of being a victim, the idea that you can't be happy without a partner or a companion, that you are not complete within yourself and that you need a soul mate to make you whole. This is true for both gay and straight relationships.

The hidden message behind the old-fashioned mother chiding her daughter to find a nice husband or Mom and friends urging their son to find a nice girl is the idea that they are not capable or good enough on their own just as they are, for surely they can't be happy, much less divine. They need someone to take care of them and make them whole. Usually more women suffer from this belief than men. I discovered to my surprise a number of years ago that I was holding that belief system when I was introduced to Ramtha through a video.

Ramtha is the Ram, the first man to ascend, from whom the Hindu religion was created. He lived thousands of years ago. In the video, Ramtha was channeled by a woman named JZ Knight. The video was of a workshop where Ramtha, through JZ, answered questions for people. One woman asked how she could have a better relationship with her husband. Ramtha started to talk about ancient times when women were either married, living in a convent, or thrown out on the streets as prostitutes, especially at a certain age when they were no longer young, attractive, or satisfying to men. He spoke of how the Persian priests had declared women to be without a soul. Consequently, men could completely dominate women and do anything to them they desired.

I sobbed through that tape, big, gut-wrenching sobs. I watched it twelve times before I could stop crying. I'm not sure if I was one of those women or one of the tyrants, but it sure struck a chord deep inside of me. Maybe I just tapped into the universal consciousness. About ten years later, I started attending Ramtha's School of Enlightenment. One afternoon during an event, he had us lying still for hours. As I was lying there, suddenly I saw FEAR OF REJECTION BY A MAN written across my forehead. I don't now remember what prompted the message, but I knew it was true, and I realized how often I would try to please a man, actually almost any person, so that I wouldn't be rejected. Maybe it was a memory from way back then. Maybe that is why a woman will stay with a man even though she is being beaten or long after she knows that it isn't right.

Painful, hidden memories stuck in our subconscious can make us do really strange things, and keep us from recognizing our divinity and attaining happiness. It took me a long time to get over the video.

My whole life has been a process of learning to speak up for myself and build self-esteem and self-confidence. Be aware that self-esteem and self-confidence come from *self*. If you have self-esteem and confidence because of another person in your life, the same individual who gives it to you can take it away in nothing flat and devastate you completely. That's why it is so important to love yourself—to look to the God within you for your love, identity, guidance, and joy. The more whole and complete you are within yourself, the happier and more loving all of your relationships will be.

Because we all project our shadow side onto others, we find so much of ourselves in the reflection. The shadow side, also called the illusion, is that nebulous part of us where we keep the feelings of guilt, shame, and negativity, as well as the memory of all those naughty things that we think that we have done, hidden from ourselves and others in the deep, dark cavern of the subconscious mind. We try to disassociate from those feelings, so we project them on other people, whom we then feel free to criticize. We attract what we are on a subconscious level. If you love and forgive yourself, you will attract love. If not, oh well, it will show you what you dislike within yourself and need to change. Look at all your relationships. What are you attracting? Are you happy?

There is a wonderful joke going around the Internet these days about the beautiful young woman sitting next to a pond. Suddenly a frog appears. He asks her to kiss him so that he can turn back into a prince. He says that he will marry her and take her to live with him and his mother in his castle where the young woman can cook and clean for him and they will live happily ever after. The end of the story finds her dining on a gourmet meal of frog legs. Cute, but a bit drastic!

Many women have already kissed Cinderella good-bye and become competent, independent, and very successful in their own right. They have become secure within themselves. These women have recognized that they are far more than just a rib and have quit looking to crawl back inside of a man to be complete. Others, the rib women, want him all to themselves. He can't look or talk to another woman without them feeling abandoned, because they are insecure and looking to him to make them feel good about themselves. "Cinderfellas," the men without a rib, try to possess a woman, and put her back inside. She belongs to him alone, and if she looks at another man, he can become enraged. In either case, the relationship generally falters.

Hopefully, we will soon see the roles of male and female as being equal expressions of the Divine. We all need to honor the caretaking role of the female and the support role of the male. I have been both a stay-at-home mom, and the sole support of my family. Believe me, it was far easier to be out in the world earning a living than it was being at home taking care of children. At home, I found that I worked all day and received no recognition for my work. Occasionally, by the time my husband came home at night, the house was in turmoil and looked as though I'd sat in front of the TV all day doing nothing but eating bonbons. Often, being a homemaker can be a thankless job.

When we honor the work our sisters do and are proud of it, the rest of the world will, as well. Luckily, today, more men are helping in the care and nurturing of children. These are little souls we are taking care of and guiding. They are the future. This role is important for humanity and the planet.

Some women in various parts of the world are still considered property and temptresses. They are hidden under burqas or veils so all you can see is their eyes. Think of the hidden message here for men. Men have no will power, no brains or discernment, and a woman can make them lose their residence in the garden. What a lot of ruckus over one lousy apple! Definitely, it's time for all of us to quit playing Adam and Eve, eating the fruit from the Tree of Knowledge of Good and evil, and start eating from the Tree of Life. If we stop blaming each other, empower ourselves, and recognize our oneness, we can reclaim our divinity, become the gods and goddesses that we truly are, have fun, and live in Paradise once again.

We can't blame all of our problems on each other, as tempting as that might be. Not all men are toads, and not all women are bitches. Women can't bemoan the fact that they were mistreated centuries ago. It's what's happening now that counts. There are plenty of princes and princesses available.

I once had a dream that stated "It's not women but men who need to know who they are." So men don't have it easy either, but they were given Superman and Prince Valiant as role models, so they had a fighting chance. Superwoman didn't come along until much later. Before that, it was Snow White and Cinderella for women—saint or victim. Wow, what a choice! Luckily there are many more choices open to most of us now. We just have to make them. Being courageous enough to go for what you want is part and parcel of reclaiming your divinity.

In some ways it's easier for women to know who they are, as their bodies give them a monthly clue. Women, see your body as a metaphor for the role of the feminine on Earth. You can bring forth life into form, feed, and nurture it. That is a sacred act. Are you seeing yourself that way? Are you manifesting your dreams? Do you honor yourself and your body? Often, women will only take care of others. They will love and nurture someone else, but not themselves.

Men, are you honoring the feminine within yourselves? Do you honor your feelings and your ideas that give form to life? Do you honor yourself and your dreams? You can love, empower yourself, and live happily ever after with or without a husband, wife, lover, partner, or significant other.

By remembering that the other person shows you your shadow side, that part of yourself that you don't want to see or acknowledge but the part that needs to be healed, you can become more aware of your life and change it. Know that the other person will manifest for you your fears, your guilt, your buried emotions, and all those wonderful things lurking in your subconscious mind. We used to call that the unconscious mind—that part of us of which we are unaware. It's the part that we don't want to deal with. It may be emotional residue from childhood, from past lives, or from painful events. We project that out onto others and it becomes our reality.

This was explained to me in a vision as follows: We are the slide or the film that is projected onto a screen. Other people and events are the screen upon which we project our shadow side, both good and bad. We learn to see ourselves in reflection and in relation to others. All life is a relationship of some sort. If you can thank others for showing you who you are and how you are behaving, no matter how much you hate it, and forgive them, the relationship can survive. You get to pass go, collect $200, and return to the Garden of Eden.

Sometimes people arrive in a relationship carrying fears and hurts from the past. They pray for someone to come into their lives to heal their wounds. Often, two needy people come together with great expectations that no earthly person can fulfill. Anger and frustration result. In general, it doesn't work. I have found that the excitement and titillation of sex and someone new may cover the wounds for a while, but soon the same old difficulties resurface and the relationship flounders. Drugs won't work—they only make the situation worse. Unless you release the old pattern and find new ways to relate, changing partners and dancing is just like changing staterooms on the Titanic. It's a sinking ship!! However, if you forgive, let go of the old pain, and learn to trust again, you can move into a new, joyous partnership.

What does work, though, is to become your own Prince/Princess Charming and be the person that you want to attract. Because like attracts like, you have to figure out what you want the other person to give you. Make a list of what is missing in your life. What do you want? Nurturing? Protection? Culture? Support? Shelter? Love? All of the above? You can have it all. Whatever it is, give it to yourself. Become your own Fairy Godmother. Love yourself enough to make of yourself all that you want to be; then what you want will come to you. All things are within you. Call them forth and become them. Imagine that you are what you want and soon they will manifest. When you aren't the needy victim anymore but the happy, empowered, divine being you wanted someone else to make you, then an individual with the qualities you want will appear. Consequently, you will be able to maintain a healthy and happy relationship that is mutually loving and supportive.

The following stories and experiences from my own life taught me the truth about myself and about relationships. They helped me move from being a frightened, neurotic young woman to a happy, empowered adult. I was married and had three lovely children. I had everything that the world says you are supposed to have in order to be happy. I had a nice husband, a nice house, a nice car, diamonds, and furs, and I was miserable. I truly was a desperate housewife, empty inside, feeling very alone in the midst of the crowd. There wasn't anything wrong with my husband or kids—it was that I didn't love myself enough or feel worthy enough to be able to receive the love that was all around me.

Trust me, no other person, food, alcohol, or drug can fill that emptiness. Only you and God can fill that, but there is hope. Hopefully with this guidance, it won't take you as long to reach happiness as it took me. I was in the dark, terrified, fumbling around, searching for the light. When my parents were divorced, I was sixteen years old. They were screaming at each other all the time. I knew that they weren't happy and none of their friends were happy, either. No one they knew understood how to be happy. I was like Diogenes looking for an honest man, only I was searching for someone who "knew" how to live happily.

I was in college and had to take a political science course in order to graduate. I wasn't the least bit interested in politics, so I took a course called "Philosophy of Government." In that class, I had to read Plato's *Republic*. It talked about people who lived in a cave and had no experience outside of the cave, so they believed that the shadows on the wall were real. It continued to teach how to set up a republic to create the greatest good for the greatest number. I finally found someone who knew! I adored the book and Plato. He was talking about the illusion and the shadow side. I knew intuitively that it was the truth, but I didn't know then that it would become a lifetime study.

I hope the stories that follow will inspire and motivate you to throw off the shackles of the past and master your life. The greatest joy comes from overcoming your limitations. You can change your life through meditation, affirmation, visualization, and forgiveness, all of which will empower you. Loving and empowering yourself go hand and hand. Remember that you can't be a victim and a master at the same time. So, look to the god or goddess within you to fulfill you. By going directly to the Source, you will never be disappointed. It's time to kiss all the victims, all the Cinderellas and Cinderfellas, good-bye for good. It's time to accept your destiny. Recognize that we are all gods and goddesses and return to the light, love, and joy in Paradise. When people want to change their lives, to grow and be happy, generally the first questions they ask are "Who am I" and "What am I doing in a mess like this?" The first step to empowerment and fun is to learn who you are. The Bowl of Truth in the next chapter demonstrates this beautifully.

chapter 2

The Bowl of Truth

Years ago, I was teaching Sunday School at the Unity Church to seventh and eighth graders. The Unity Church, part of The Unity School of Christianity, is based on the precept that there is only One Presence and One Power, God the Good, Omniscient. I asked Spirit, that part of God that knows where we are and what we need in order to recognize our oneness, to show me a way to help the students understand this principle. I saw a vision of a bowl of water with some objects in it. I thought it was quite clever, as Spirit always is, and I could hardly wait to see how the idea would work out. I placed a clear crystal bowl filled almost to the top with water in front of my students and told them to imagine that the bowl was filled with water and there was nothing else in the Universe. I told them to imagine that in reality the bowl did not exist, as there was nothing limiting the water. I asked them to tell me what they saw.

They started to call out words such as stuff, water, infinity, forever, creation, peace, and Heaven. I encouraged them to go further and they came up with Spirit, life, The All, love, and God. I questioned them even further. What was Spirit? What was The All? And what was God? After quite a few ums and uhs, one brave soul said, "Well, if there isn't anything else, then it has to be everything, everywhere, and has to have created everything in the bowl, and for sure it is smart. If it is The All, then all the different words had to be the same thing—life, Spirit, forever, God, love, and Heaven."

I asked them what about Hell? After a few more ums, they decided that if the bowl was everything, then Hell had to be there as well. Then one of them asked what made the difference between Heaven and Hell if it was all the same stuff? A third student said, "How about what you think about it?" Most of them agreed, but a few said that Heaven and Hell had to be different. Some said that if it was all the same stuff and that's all there was, it couldn't be different.

While they were continuing to debate the issue, I placed some objects in the water. Among them was a silver bowl, two brightly colored sake cups, two white china cups, a crystal wine glass, and a little plastic cup. Again I asked the students to tell me what they saw. The answers were varied: "They're all different on the outside, but they're all filled with the same stuff." "Some had more than others." "The form was different." "The containers were mostly different." "Some were big, while others were small." Some held a lot of water, while others had just a little, but they all were there in the same bowl together. "They were just like people." That was as far as I went with the children.

The second time I did the bowl exercise was for *A Course in Miracles* class. Each time I did the bowl exercise, more was revealed. *A Course in Miracles* is a three-volume work that was channeled in the 1970s by Helen Schucman, a professor of medical psychology at Columbia University's College of Physicians and Surgeons. She and her fellow workers were having difficulty getting along; they thought that they should have better relationships because they were psychologists, but they didn't. When the boss demanded that they learn to get along, fellow psychologist Bill Thetford joined Schucman in seeking a better way. I imagine that they prayed for guidance.

One day Schucman heard a voice say, "This is a Course in Miracles . . . " For seven years, she continued to hear the voice until the book was complete. Thetford helped her with the project and *A Course in Miracles* was born. The essence of it is: there is nothing but God. Anything else that we are seeing is an illusion, unreal, just the images of our own projections. When we look into a bowl of water, all we see is our own reflection. The way to move from the illusion to reality is through forgiveness and the recognition of our oneness with God.

I started with the same premise, a bowl of water, then added the cups, then asked the class what they thought the plastic cup, thought about the silver bowl. One of them said that the silver bowl makes the plastic cup feel inferior—the silver bowl definitely is richer and snobby. Another imagined that the silver bowl thought it was high and mighty. The plastic cup definitely came from the wrong side of the tracks, but the silver cup was denser and stuck on the bottom while the plastic cup could float up to the surface. Because it was floating higher in the bowl, it thought it was more spiritual than the silver bowl.

"What about the brightly colored sake cups, How would they feel toward the plain white cups?" I asked. "Oh, they are so much happier than those plain cups. They are so ordinary, whereas the sake cups are colorful, joyous, lively, and having so much fun," said one student. "The white cups are quite leery of the show-off sake cups. They need so much attention. They are always so brightly colored," said another student.

I suggested that the students listen quietly and maybe they could hear what the objects were saying about each other. We were quite surprised at what we heard. "I don't want to be in the same place as you. We don't want to be with those kind of people. The show-offs feel the plain Janes are just too boring for them. Nobody talks to the crystal glass; he's so high and mighty. He's purer than we are, you know. He's bigger and mightier. God, I wish I were like him."

"Oh, stop whining, you stupid plastic cup. Don't you know that you have the same substance within you that I do?" said the crystal wine glass.

"But you have more than I do."

"It doesn't matter how much you have within you. Even a drop of the substance that I like to call God is all the same in everyone. It makes you wise and all knowing. All knowledge is within you, if you look to the substance within you rather than continually complaining that you are only a little plastic cup. What difference does it make? That's just your ego, the part of you that's scared, that feels alone even though you have the mightiest force in the world right under your nose," continued the wine cup.

"I don't have a nose."

"Oh, yeah, sorry, but Plastic Cup, you have the same stuff, the same life force within you if you honor it and let it guide you and love you."

"Love?"

"Yes, Cup, the life force is love. Start honoring yourself, realizing that you are a wonderful cup filled with all that is powerful in the Universe. When you start to look to what is within you and know that's who you really are, maybe you will quit complaining and have a lot more fun. So what do you think of that?"

"Love, hmmmm. Do you mean that all this stuff around me that I'm swimming in is just love?"

"Just love? My boy, love is the greatest power there is, so be grateful for it. It's the only thing that's important. The only thing that's real."

"Oh, yeah?"

"Yes, little cup. It's true. All the rest is just what you think about it, the projection from your own mind onto your Universe. Once you begin to let go of your past ideas, forgive them so to speak, you only see love and know that you are swimming in a Universe of unconditional love."

"Hey, Mr. Wine Glass, you really are smart!"

"You would be as smart as I am if you looked to the substance within instead of being concerned with how everyone else looks, and comparing yourself to them. Know that you are all one, containers for the same energy, or the substance that is everything."

"One? But there are lots of us in the bowl."

"Right, but remember that everyone is filled with the same life force. So everyone is the same."

"Hey that's a great thing, but it sure doesn't look that way."

"Look a little deeper. Try harder to see the truth within other containers. When you realize that you are far greater than just a container or ego, there is nothing you cannot do."

"Hey, thanks, Crystal Wine Glass. I'm happy to be sharing this bowl with you."

"Well, thank you White Cup. When you two white cups can feel the same way about the whiny, plastic cup, that's when you will recognize The Truth."

"But you're crystal."

"What did I just tell you? Quit comparing and criticizing and just look for the love and you will find it everywhere, especially within yourself. You're swimming in it! We're all swimming in it! When you hold tight to your container and think that is all you are, you're missing all the fun. Spread out. Recognize that you are part of everything around you. Look at the substance not the form and be free. It's that simple."

"It can't be that simple."

"But it is."

Consciousness and Energy

I had a great epiphany recently in a Reiki class I was teaching at a local school. It showed me a deeper level of the workings of oneness, consciousness, and the bowl. *Reiki* means Universal Life Energy. Rei means soul and Ki means energy. It is a Japanese laying-on-of-hands healing modality that I have been teaching since 1984, but this class was different. Because the students were to be certified by the state, the classes needed to be longer than the usual Reiki classes for some reason. I walked in and said to the students, "This is the longest living Reiki class in captivity." I believed that my Reiki classes were already longer than most Reiki teachers' classes to begin with. In this class, I had five more students than I usually do, and the school was temporarily housed in the basement of a bank because the massage school was building a new school.

The students had to walk down a long corridor to find the place where I was doing the initiations, which meant that everything would take longer. There are four initiations to the energy in a beginning Reiki class. The initiations attune the students to their soul energy. The attunements or initiations create a generator in their aura or energy field that allows them to heal others as well as themselves. Each initiation takes about five minutes. Getting them in and out of the room can extend the time.

There were several different groups from different cities in the class. Some insisted upon being attuned together, which made it difficult for my assistants and added greatly to the time involved. Between the temporary housing problem and the few difficult students, the class ended about an hour and a half longer than planned.

We picked Angel Cards in class. These are little cards with pictures of an angel and a word on it. I like to use them, as they give the students a focus for their healing in the class. I picked the word "PLAY" . . . play??? I had never worked so hard in all my life! Usually, no matter how many students, no matter the language, all students are cooperative, eager, and willing. Yet some of these students were arbitrary and difficult to attune. I definitely wasn't having any fun!

I went home hopping mad and determined to change the energy. The next day I brought my crystal bowl attuned to the heart center, which I knew would open their hearts. My crystal bowls are made entirely of glass, and when the edges are rubbed with a striker, a stick covered with a suede fabric, they make a beautiful sound that will transform the energy. I instructed the class and my assistants that there should be four students at the door ready to enter for their attunements when the previous four who were already attuned left to go back to resume healing.

This would speed up the process, and everyone had to work with new partners or else!!! I felt like General Patton, determined to move my army to glory. It worked! It all moved easily. The students became easy to attune and their energy was beautiful! They were filled with light, and the class ended on time!!!! What a tremendous difference from the day before.

It wasn't until the next morning while I was contemplating the class and my Angel Card that I realized that the Reiki class was the "PLAY" of my consciousness. Like does attract like, as I had stated first thing in the morning that it was the longest living Reiki class in captivity, and Spirit made it happen. I really didn't mean for that to be my intention, but it obviously was my belief, as that was the manifestation. The subconscious mind does not have a sense of humor. Because we are all one, the class manifested that for me. Spirit showed me what my feelings were.

I witnessed it in the few disgruntled students. When I changed my mind and my attitude, my consciousness changed and the class became as lovely as all the others had been. It was amazing to me to see what happened when I finally became clear.

Everything truly is an illusion! It isn't real, just a reflection of your consciousness. That's a reason to be joyous! If you're not having fun, change it, and come from the divinity within you, which is always love peace and joy. Change your mind and your attitude, and you change your consciousness. When you do, you will attract something completely different. When the light dawns and you finally realize what you have created, it does become hysterically funny! The worst of it is that you can't blame anyone else. It's all you, baby! Look around you and see your play – your drama – your creation.

It all represents you on one level and God on a deeper level. The beauty of that is you can change it the minute you don't like what is going on. Ramtha used to say, "ATTITUDE IS EVERYTHING." Attitude does create your perception of reality. I actually witnessed the illusion in action. I did confess to my class on Sunday after their third attunement, and told them how beautiful their energy was. It showed me that it's what you are that creates your life, not just what you focus on, but your thoughts and feelings, as well. I thought I had recognized that before, but not at all to this degree. Pay attention to your environment. It all represents you. It *is* all about you! Create a beautiful life that brings light, love, peace, and joyous blessings to all. Love yourself enough to allow yourself to be who you really are, the water, not the container. That is your destiny!

I, Too, Had a Dream

A little while ago when I was rewriting this book for the fortieth time, I had this dream: I was taking a class from another woman. She started the class and I knew that she didn't know how to finish it. I asked her if she wanted me to teach the second half of the class. She agreed and drove me there. We went up a large hill.

When I looked out, there was nothing there. It looked as though we were going out into space and then we went straight down the other side of the hill. She went slowly enough so that it wasn't a problem. I complemented her on her driving and said in the dream that I was so excited, I could hardly wait to hear what I would say. I said to the students that I was really excited because I never before had the freedom to teach a class with no parameters, and I continued to say, "You were created in the image of God. You are what you were created to be. When you came in to your parents' world, they had all their hopes and dreams, for themselves and for you. Sometimes they can be angry if they didn't achieve their dreams and you did. We're going to take away the stuff that you and society have placed upon you that has covered up the original idea of being created in the image of God."

I could hardly wait to go to sleep the next night to find out what happened in the rest of the class. I was disappointed that I didn't receive any more information, but it did let me know how we can reclaim our divinity. Since we all are as we were created to be, we haven't lost it, we've just buried it under all the "I'm not good enoughs," "I can'ts," "shoulds," "oughts," and "I don't knows," or stuffed it in a container trying to live up to society's demands that we be nurses when we really want to be mechanics, or astronauts.

You are a divine being, one with God. You are good enough, You can do anything. Within you is all knowledge and all power. Start affirming what you truly are and see what happens.

Call it forth. Allow yourself to manifest the truth, to be what you really are, to do what you really want. Go for it! Do what will make you happy. Don't waste your time looking for someone else to give it to you. Someone else can't do it for you. Do, though, look for people who support your efforts to be all you can be, people who are doing it for themselves. Then you will attract a valuable partner.

PART II

How to Get Rid of the Heebie-Jeebies

chapter 3

Releasing Fear

Remembering who we are, beings filled with the light, love, and intelligence of Spirit, is that simple. But it is often difficult to do when we find ourselves hiding from our illusions deep down in our containers, frightened and feeling separate from our source, from everyone else, and from the rest of the world. Fear will make us hold tight to our container. Ego or personality are other names for the container. We compare ourselves to others, compete with them, judge them, criticize them, and often come off wanting. When we are afraid, we don't feel the love, protection, and security that is all around.

We forget who we are, and the truth – that we are one with Spirit, God, The All, the Life Force, or whatever you choose to call the water. (I use all of the terms interchangeably; if you don't like one, choose one you do like. Often people have big hang-ups with the word "God" from their past programming.) All we feel is fear. It takes the fun out of life and makes us do all sorts of strange things. One of my favorite sayings is, "When you're up to your ass in alligators, it's difficult to remember that the initial objective was to drain the swamp." So the second step out of the quagmire is to get rid of fear and anxiety. Once we release our fear, it is so much easier to recognize the divinity within ourselves and others.

Comparisons: The Ticket to Hell

I went to a Ramtha Intensive back in the 1980s. It was held in Seattle at the Red Lion Inn. There were about 350 people in the room, and when I returned from lunch, I found there were only two seating options left, either the back row where I couldn't see anything or the floor near the stage. I opted for the floor so that I could see.

At the end of the day, Ramtha walked through a door directly in front of me, turned around, and came and kissed the man standing next to me. He told the man how happy he was that he was there. I started to do my thing. My thing was, "There must be something the matter with me or he would have picked me instead of the man next to me. I'm not good enough, etc., etc., etc."

Suddenly in the midst of all that, I heard myself say, "NO, I'm not going to do that to myself one more time." I realized that what Ramtha did with the man standing next to me had nothing to do with me unless I chose to put myself in the middle of it, unless I chose to compare myself to him.

Comparison is the ticket to Hell. Do not pass go, do not collect $200, go directly to Hell! If you compare yourself to someone and come off superior today, you're sure to find yourself inferior to someone else tomorrow. It never ends. Actually, we are all unique, and it's like comparing apples and oranges on the physical level of what appears to be. It's a giant leap back to the container. On a more spiritual level, we are all the same divine beings created by a loving Father/Mother God.

Remember, you are not who you think you are, you are not who they think you are, but you are what you think they think you are. Whatever you are projecting on others and saying that is what they think about you is what you really feel about yourself. As it says in *A Course in Miracles,* "The truth in you remains as radiant as a star, as pure light, as innocent as love itself." You are not what you think you are or what others have taught you about yourself. You are as you were created to be.

I had to work all night to not put myself down and stay out of Hell. The next morning, I came into the room early. I picked up a glass of water from the back of the room and found a seat. I looked up and saw Ramtha laughing at me. I toasted him with my water glass, and for one moment I felt equal to that glorious being. It was divine! He would always say about himself, "I am Ramtha, the Enlightened One." How's that for an affirmation? Try it!

At the same conference, I met a young man whom I shall call Bob. We were dining together and he told me his story. About a year prior to the event, Bob was worried about his teaching ability, suddenly feeling that others were better or more competent than he. He was a teacher of metaphysics and was feeling as though he should quit the business. As he was driving home from class one evening, he was considering giving it all up.

That night he had the following dream: He dreamt about a beautiful mountain. There were paths going around the mountain everywhere, and people were on the paths. Some people were together on a path and some were alone, but all of them had one thing in common. Each held a placard—some signs were large, some small, some very ornate, some plain—but all of the signs said the very same thing. All said, **"Follow me."**

He realized then that all of the people in his life had tried to influence him with their ideas and belief systems, saying that what they knew and understood was best or better than anyone else, certainly better than what he knew. After that dream, he gained confidence in his own knowingness and he decided to continue to teach.

One of the most difficult lessons to learn is that the Kingdom of Heaven is within, to trust that your own inner guidance—that the God within you knows what is best for you, no matter what anyone else says, and that your own knowingness is right for you. Trust it! No Matter What.

Make a list of all the people you think are smarter, holier, more loving, or more important than you. List what talent, beauty, or grace they have that you feel you don't have. Affirm: We are all one. It is only an illusion that we are separate individuals. The same God that is within that individual is within me. I am that individual. Feel what it feels like to be that individual and have those attributes. Affirm that you have all that you need, and know what is right for you.

Another little visit to Hell came when I went to a psychic fair. I was only there to promote my Reiki class, but Carol, the woman running the fair, asked me if I would do readings, because three people had called in sick. A reading is done either with cards, an astrology chart, or just by giving the person your intuitive impressions. I agreed to do them and did a number of readings throughout the day.

At the end of the day, she asked me if I would do readings again at the fair the following month. I agreed, and then began to panic. I felt that one out of the twenty readings I did wasn't that great, and for sure I wasn't as good a reader as some of my friends. Finally it dawned on me that the same energy that did the readings in my friends was also in me, and if I allowed it to work through me, instead of being in fear, I could do fabulous readings as well. I continued to affirm that for the month and the second fair turned out beautifully. Spirit within us can do anything if we let it. Fear will stop everything!

Avoid the temptation to compare at all costs. It will very quickly move you away from The Truth about yourself and wreak havoc. You will have to work hard to pull yourself out of Hell.

When I was a teenager, my mother became quite frightened and very difficult to live with after her divorce. Life with her was like living with a land mine—I never knew what step would blow up in my face, as what was right yesterday was not necessarily going to be okay today. I was punished all the time and became very frightened. All this created a lot of anxiety in me. It did, however, start me on a quest to find out how to live and be happy. That search took me on quite a ride.

About that time, I had a dream. I was in high school then. I dreamed that I was tied to a mill wheel face up. It was going around in circles. As it came down to the ground, I would go under water, then come up toward the sky, and continue around the circle again and again and again. It was horrible! I remember it as an old-fashioned-looking wheel. I think it was used to grind grain in the olden days. At the end of the dream, I said, "I have to get off of this wheel." Because it was frightening, I remembered the dream distinctly. It would be a long time until I understood the dream, but it made a big impression on me.

The wheel represented the wheel of life and the cycle of death and rebirth that goes on forever until we realize that we are divine beings and climb off the wheel—or out of our containers—to live eternally.

Another experience that got my attention as a teenager boggled my mind. I was cleaning out my closet, and suddenly I had a revelation. I didn't know what that was then, but a weird sensation went through my body and I became very present. I realized that trees were alive, flowers were alive, and I was alive. I wondered what would happen to me when I wasn't anymore. It was my first recognition of the life force within me and in all things. I had no clue what was happening to me. Years later, when I shared my story with a teacher, he told me that I'd had a spiritual experience. I didn't know what that meant either, but it added to my uneasiness and fear.

A Principle of Aikido

Bow to your enemies and honor them, for they are
the surface upon which you polish yourself.

At one of the Reiki Master conferences, we had an introduction to Aikido, where I learned that principle. It taught me that there is only one relationship, the one between you and your divine self, as everything else is an illusion. We project onto others what we see within ourselves, and that image reflects out from us like ripples in a pond, or the bowl, as the case may be. As we struggle with our projections and finally forgive them, we polish ourselves. I have seen the enemy and it is I. While I was doing yoga, I saw the enemy in a spontaneous past-life regression.

In the midst of lying on the floor doing the postures, I suddenly felt as though I were a man lying in the dirt. I could smell the dirt in my nostrils. I looked up and saw golden, onion-shaped domes above me and said aloud, "The Brahmans won't let me in the temple." I started to sob from the depths of my soul and realized that I was a man, an "untouchable," in India. The anguish of being a rejected outcast, dirty and unwanted, flowed through me. It was the most horrible feeling I have ever experienced. I lay there and sobbed for hours. At that moment, the "untouchable" was more real than the "Nancy" I thought I was at that time. I even got up in the middle of the experience and called a friend of mine to tell her what happened to me. After the call, I lapsed back into those feelings and continued to sob. I had been at the Meditation Institute where they taught me how to meditate and do past life regressions, but this happened spontaneously.

The experience took me back to a prior time in my life. I call my early years the years of the Heebie-Jeebies—you know, that state of being where fear and anxiety rule, your brain becomes like jelly, and the bogeyman dances in your shadow. I was nervous, neurotic, phobic, and suffering from anxiety attacks all the time. I was afraid of everyone and everything. I battled with fear most of my adult life.

As a very young child, I had no fear at all. My mother told me that at the tender age of five, I would take off all my clothes and run naked through the neighborhood in the wee, small hours of the morning. The naked streaker would arise in me and want to be free at interesting times. I don't run naked around the neighborhood anymore, but I would have enormous bouts of courage arise, if need be.

The rest of the time I was in fear. Most of the time, I was living the life of Nancy on the surface, but I had the subconscious feelings of an "untouchable." The experience brought to light many things: I always expected to be rejected. I can remember holding back, cautiously waiting to see if I would be welcomed wherever I went. The experience explained the years of being in the midst of wealth, but not having any money personally. I was given a clothing allowance at the age of eleven. The amount never changed from that age to the day I got married. What was a lot of money at age eleven was hardly anything at twenty-one! I never felt I had the right to ask for more money; I just made do with what I had. It was difficult for me to ask anyone for a favor, as well.

In retrospect, I realize that for the next twenty years, I was healing the "untouchable" and all those other wonderful characters—Dopey, Sleepy, and Goofy— lurking in my subconscious mind. Our minds work the same as computers. The conscious mind is like the computer programmer. It decides what we like or don't like, and directs our energy accordingly. It is the part that sets goals and makes plans. It represents the active, masculine part of us. All of those directives then go into the subconscious mind, and are usually forgotten. It is like the hard drive. On the other hand, the subconscious is the receptive, deductive part of our mind that is akin to the feminine part of us. Our subconscious minds also hold our original programming by Spirit where we know that we are healed, perfect, and one with God—where all is one. It is the intuitive part of us and has been called the deeper, or supra-conscious, mind.

When we are frightened or difficult things happen to us, we lose our connection to the divine part of us, and we override our original programming with thoughts of revenge, anger, hatred, and so on. This separated part of us is known as the ego, or the container in the Bowl of Truth. We can access these deeper parts of our mind through meditation and reprogramming, which will be discussed in subsequent chapters. Suppressed feelings become the bogeymen that lie there in our subconscious, waiting to literally scare us to death. Whenever something happens in our lives that we can't let go of, we retain it in our subconscious mind. They used to call it our unconscious mind, that part of us we are not aware of. The subconscious or unconscious makes up ninety percent of us and is reflected in the people and events around us—the containers in the bowl. That becomes the illusion because we are all one in reality. We are only seeing our own thoughts and feelings reflected upon them. Like attracts like, and we are seeing in others what we love or dislike in ourselves. We say that opposites attract, but opposites are only extremes of the same thing.

I have a son who is my exact opposite astrologically. As he was growing up, we always wanted to do the exact opposite thing in the very same place. I would clean the house all day and sit down to meditate just as he would come in and say, "You've been here all day, now I'm here to crank tunes." The very thing I hated! It was horrible for both of us! A friend pointed out to me what was happening, and finally we could laugh about it when we would both arrive in the bathroom to take a shower at a time when neither of us were supposed to be there, asking one another in surprised voices, "What are you doing here?"

My son has taught me how to trust and be flexible. Today, when I'm in the midst of cooking a meal and the phone rings, I always know who it is, but we also share many other things and wonderful events in nature, as well. One day, I was talking to him on the phone just as a mama duck took her babies to our pond for their first swim. We talked for hours as I excitedly described the event that we both enjoyed. Now we share *A Course in Miracles*, as well. It's wonderful!

The subconscious mind is the feminine side of our being, the emotional, feeling side. It represents the women in our lives and the self. It's the memory, or what's in the hard drive. It also links us with universal knowledge and Spirit. Disturbing emotions, if left a long time to fester, become diseases, so we need to transmute our fears and release anger, guilt, and negativity.

The conscious mind represents the masculine part of our being, the computer programmer, others, and the men in our lives. If we're all one, we all have the "Untouchable" within us as well as the master, and all parts of humanity. It's all there in the bowl. Some just focus on the "Untouchable," or other horrible aspects, more than others. What we focus on, we create. Astrology will show us what we choose to experience in this lifetime. Low self-esteem, dysfunction, and challenges will show up in an astrology chart. Some prefer to think of it as a haphazard, random act of fate; I choose to think of it as a choice of my soul. We choose the situation that best describes the set-up in our mind in order to release whatever is limiting us, to know we are one with God, The All.

Releasing and forgiving that which limits us is healing. The limitations that we have been born with, whether they be emotional, physical, or mental, are only illusions, not our true selves. In the process of healing ourselves, enlightenment is the result. In the search for enlightenment, healing is the result.

You don't have to know about past lives or even believe in them to heal yourself. You are the sum total of everything you have ever been, right now. You are all things and all people. You are the untouchable and the murderer, as well as the genius, the Master, and the angel. Remember the bowl. We are all divine beings. Knowing that we are all divine beings unites the duality in us forever. All relationships are only seeing ourselves in reflection.

I have decided that it doesn't matter if there is such a thing as past lives. Life is eternal. We are all one and it may just be our subconscious' way of giving us a symbolic picture of how we feel now. By seeing such images as a past life, may be easier for us to deal with. It gives us a little perspective. Actually, everything up to this second is the past. Each time one of these feelings comes up, we have to change our fears to love until we love all beings unconditionally, or we can never love ourselves. It isn't about someone else; it's only about us. Life is all about returning to the center, the source of all things.

Learning how to quell the fear, quiet down, and unite the male and female aspects is the task. When conscious and subconscious quit battling and learn to love and be loved, the illusions disappear and there's nothing left but Divinity. Spirit is now free to manifest the treasure within, and you become a joyous light to the world.

Triumph over Terror

Like Dorothy in *The Wizard of Oz*, we all want to go home. Unfortunately, we have to find our loving hearts, wisdom, and the courage to allow our true selves to emerge before we can manifest Heaven on Earth. Other people mirror for us what's hidden in our subconscious minds. They show us what we haven't forgiven within ourselves. By forgiving them or letting those past hurts go, we forgive and heal ourselves. It took me a long time to recognize this. I was so afraid that I would look at everyone else and think that they were perfect and that I was the only one who was afraid and had problems.

As a young girl, I tried to appear as perfect as I thought everyone else was. In those days (months, years), I did a lot of things to be accepted and I lied a lot. I never told anyone what was happening to me or how I felt. It never occurred to me that I was afraid and that my body reacted to the fear by having anxiety attacks. People have stomach aches, heart palpitations, difficulty breathing, or whatever they create to express the terror they feel inside. Mine were minor at first, but the more I became afraid an anxiety attack would happen again, the more it happened. It turned into a vicious cycle.

Sometimes I would be nervous in the beginning of a class, or at parties, restaurants, or any event. It didn't seem to matter what it was. Most of the time, I created anxiety attacks before an event by worrying about it on the way to a place or by being afraid it would happen again. Eventually, the anxiety calmed down, and slowly I felt better. Most of the time it would all go away, and I could forget my fear and have a good time, but I was always afraid that the anxiety would return.

It wasn't until recently that I discovered that rehearsing the past keeps it alive in the present and recreates it in the future.

By the time I reached my late twenties with all that going on, I began to fear leaving the house. I had created agoraphobia, the fear of open spaces. I was quite adept at covering it all up, and looked pretty cool on the outside, so no one knew anything was wrong with me, except that I might make seventy-five trips to the bathroom on the way to a place, or have to leave a place abruptly. It was very important for me to be **perfect!** It was important to keep it all *hidden.* Keeping feelings hidden make them more frightening, and I started praying for help. I was constantly asking for guidance and help out of the prison I had created. I received four powerful messages. The first message I heard was: LET THE DUALITY OF GEMINI BE UNITED IN YOU.

Sometime later, the second message arrived when I heard: RETURN TO THE CENTER THE SOURCE OF ALL THINGS.

A few years down the road, when I really was begging for assurance, Spirit told me: YOU HAVE TO BE QUIET IF YOU WANT TO ENTER THE SANCTUARY. That has been quite difficult to do.

I have been working with these messages for years. Just when I think that I've achieved them, I uncover another layer to master. It's a continuous adventure, and not always fun, mind you, being led and guided by Spirit from fear and separation to the goal of love, mastery, and oneness.

The fourth message came in a dream. It looked like energy going round and round straight in front of me like a spinning wheel standing on end moving rapidly in a circular motion. All that I could see was the rear view of the wheel. I wasn't quite sure what I was looking at but the message with that vision was: EVERYTHING IS GOING 'ROUND IN CIRCLES. YOU HAVE TO STRAIGHTEN IT OUT AND THEN IT DROPS DOWN.

I felt that "drops down" meant that it would then manifest on the physical level. I really had no idea what that meant until I went to the Meditation Institute. I saw a sign on the wall with a picture of a skeleton key, which opens most locks, was what I had seen in my dream, except I had seen it from the rear view, and it said "Know thyself."

Suddenly I knew what I was being told. If I would focus on what I wanted, straighten out my mind and my thoughts, then it could all manifest. That was the key to life. How simple!!! I had forgotten the dream about the mill wheel by that time, but the message is remarkably similar.

It wasn't until years later that I heard of the concept that **consciousness and energy create the nature of reality** and began to understand the process.

Whatever you focus on, you can create. The Kahunas, ancient Hawaiian healers, say everything is affected by our perception of it. We find what we expect to find. I realized that my fear of having another anxiety attack was my focus, and thus I was constantly recreating such attacks.

The principles of the Kahunas, or Huna, are important tools for transformation. They are:

1. Ike-The world is what you think it is.

2. Kala-There are no limits.

3. Makia-Energy flows where attention goes.

4. Manawa-Now is the moment of power.

5. Aloha-To love is to be happy with.

6. Mana-All power comes from within.

7. Pono-Effectiveness is the measure of truth.

I finally understood how I created the entire process of fear, anxiety attacks, and phobias, and had to slowly un-create it through breathing exercises, affirmations, visualization, and meditation techniques. Hindsight can bring great wisdom. It was a long, slow process learning to quiet down. I could have ended the anxiety a lot sooner if I had put **ALL** of my focus on being healed instead of half of it. At that time, I spent half the time being afraid the attacks would happen again and the other half doing all of the techniques to overcome the fear. I was polarized between balancing the 'fraidy cat on the one hand and the naked streaker on the other. There was that duality again.

Spirit gently guided me step by step through Concept Therapy, meditation, affirmations, *A Course in Miracles,* and Reiki to heal me. Concept Therapy teaches that there is nothing but God and energy in the world and they are one and the same, thus uniting science and religion. The ideas you have create the form for the energy to fill. Therefore, everything begins with an idea and you create your own reality. Does that sound familiar? It's the same principle as the bowl and *Ike*—the world is what you think it is.

People tell me today that they can't believe I was that afraid. Anything can be changed. If I could change, you can change. It will be easier for you because you have all the information on how to transform. There is so much in print today. They discuss panic attacks in the newspaper, but thirty years ago people didn't talk about *that.* I was standing on the edge of Hell, groping in the dark, praying for help. I had to forge a new path.

Today, with all of my accumulated "pearls of wisdom," I would make a joke about a panic attack incident, let it go, and be done with it! The whole process could take a total of ten minutes instead of thirty years. Of course, that would have been the end of a promising career as a healer. When I finally realized that overcoming the panic attacks led me to my spiritual growth, I became grateful for them. Gratitude made them all disappear. We all have fears; the more we can make light of them, the easier they are to bear. We can't let them destroy us, and we can transmute them.

They say that angels can fly because they take themselves very lightly. At that time in my life I was sinking and going lower all the time. Lightly, what was that???

Let me give you another example of how consciousness and energy create the nature of reality. This was proven to me in an interesting way about how our minds work. I had been teaching in Japan for a number of years, going there twice a year. On one of my trips, my travel agent booked a return ticket through Seattle. I was supposed to arrive in Seattle at 8:50 a.m. and leave on a direct flight to Milwaukee at 10:05. From the moment I saw the ticket, I was certain that I didn't have enough time to make the connection, and started planning to take the next flight, which left at 11:40 with a change in Minneapolis. I told my husband, Ray, that I would call him from Minneapolis to tell him what time I would actually arrive. My mind or consciousness had already decided that I was going to miss the 10:05 flight and would probably be on the 11:40, but I was not aware of what I was doing then.

The plane landed exactly on time at 8:50 a.m. We breezed through customs. When I went to get my suitcase, I thought I saw it come up on the carousel, but I never saw it come around to me. I did have a passing thought that maybe someone had taken it off the carousel, as that had happened to me once before in Boston. I was busy talking to a woman who was moving back to the States about all the boxes she had. I didn't go look for my suitcase, as I figured that I had all the time in the world . . . since I was going to miss the 10:05 flight.

Suddenly a man in a red jacket came up to me and asked if I had found my suitcase. I told him that I hadn't, and he informed me that he had taken a number of them off the carousel and placed them on the other side of the room. I walked over with him to see if mine was there. Sure enough, there it was! I picked it up, went through customs, and walked immediately through a door to hand my suitcase to the transfer agent. I missed my plane by five minutes!

It was such a shock to me that it made me aware of my whole process. If I had spent half the time saying that I could make the 10:05 flight, perhaps I would have acted on the message I received—that someone might have taken my suitcase off the carousel. What good is intuition if you don't follow it? P.S. I hadn't seen a man in a red jacket either before or after at that baggage carousel.

The airline no longer has a direct 10:05 flight to Milwaukee. I wonder, did the Universe have to create that man in the red jacket just to show me how consciousness and energy create the nature of reality, just to make sure that I missed that plane??? After all, it was my intention! It proved to me how important it is to focus on what you DO want. In retrospect, I realized that he walked straight over to me, and didn't ask anyone else.

A ridiculous story perhaps, but it was a valuable lesson in my life on how the mind works. In the Seth material, books channeled by Jane Roberts, Seth talks about how we create our own reality. It says that the Universe is constantly arranging and rearranging itself according to our definition of reality. I found that concept to be true. Watch out for little men in red jackets!

It's important to be aware of your thoughts and what you say. Your words will tell you what you think. They can make you or break you, which reminds me of a story about a friend of mine who came into town and told me that she was looking for a place to crash. She called me a week later to say that she had found a place, fell down the stairs, and broke her arm. Be careful of what you ask for! What we say, we invoke. Our subconscious mind does not have a sense of humor. It is very literal. Give it proper directions!

Today you can read about phobias in the newspaper, but in the fifties, sixties, and early seventies, people were still into hiding everything, especially abuse and compulsive behaviors, and pretending that everything was FINE. Today people are telling everything they know or ever have done on TV talk shows. Sometimes I wonder which is worse. Maybe soon we can have some kind of middle ground.

If asked how I was then, with teeth clenched, I'd say, "FINE." If asked what was the matter, I would say with a grim expression, especially with teeth and everything else clenched, "NOTHING!" I was not into my emotions. I never shared my feelings. They were something I was trying to get over or change. I thought it wasn't spiritual to be angry, so I wouldn't be. I tried to repress my feelings. Mostly, I would what is affectionately known as "stuff" them. I thought I was very loving, but I really was very angry and resentful. I was going to be **SPIRITUAL** by God, even if it killed me! I had the idea that it wasn't spiritual to say NO to anyone about anything, so I didn't.

I also thought it wasn't spiritual to talk to anyone about money, so I never did. It was just as difficult to say you owe me ten cents as it was to say you owe me ten thousand dollars. I always felt that I should overcome my feelings and be more spiritual.

When a partner and I were designing games in the seventies, several men had created a board game of their own. They wanted to buy ours as well, with the idea of starting a company. They were supposed to give us $350 up front to show their good will. They never paid us the money, and our attorney wanted us to ask that the game be returned. We, of course, thought it wasn't "spiritual" to ask for the money they owed us. "It's only money," was our excuse. Eventually they went out of business in another city. All their property, including our game, was locked up. We ended up paying another attorney in that city a fortune to get our game back. Years later, it occurred to me that had we demanded that they uphold their end of the contract and pay us the money they owed, maybe they wouldn't have invested in a

TV commercial and gone out of business. Perhaps we would all be in business today. It's important that people uphold their contracts and do what they say they will do. That is spiritual behavior. It's called "walking your talk." Contracts come in all sorts of packages. Do what you say you will do, and if you can't for some reason, say so. That's spiritual.

Back then, I couldn't stand up for myself in any way, whether it be for money or anything else. I will never forget the first time I did. I was standing in the check-out line at the grocery store and realized I was holding a half-rotten cucumber. I decided for the first time in my life that I wasn't going to accept it. I was standing there shaking inside when I said to the clerk, "I don't want to pay thirty-five cents for this." Prior to that it was, "Oh well, it's only thirty-five cents, three hundred and fifty dollars, ten thousand, or any amount—it's only money" until I no longer had any. The clerk said, "I don't blame you." God did not strike me dead! The store was still standing, and I began to feel good about myself.

Since then, it has been a continual process of learning how to stand up for myself, to honestly confront people and issues, and to say how I feel. It has been a long, hard journey learning to be assertive, not aggressive, but it was an important part of my healing process. It was a necessary step to becoming quiet. When I began to speak up and create boundaries for myself, the world became a much safer place, and I wasn't as frightened or angry It did wonders for my self-esteem!

Counselor and author John Bradshaw in his books has given a name to all this. He calls it "toxic shame." Toxic shame, which comes from being raised in a dysfunctional atmosphere, is the feeling of not being good enough just as we are. This creates the feeling of shame with all sorts of compulsive, addictive behaviors, such as substance abuse, to cover up how we feel. Sometimes we need to be perfect, or we work to excess, to camouflage what we really feel inside.

One day, very early in the ballgame, I was standing in my living room with tears rolling down my face. I was aware that I had everything that life had to offer, but I was miserable, unfulfilled, and terribly afraid of life. I thought I was crazy! I thought the rest of the world was perfect and I was the only one who wasn't. I stood there asking, "Dear God, what's the matter with me?" The answer began to unfold slowly over the next thirty years. The answer was FEAR. When I found *A Course in Miracles*, I realized that changing fear into love was the healing process. I remember sitting in the audience in a theater shaking in my boots and thinking that if just one person could not be afraid, imagine what that person could do for the world.

Years later, when I thought I had finally overcome all the nervousness and neurotic behavior, it all came back in a flash one day—anxiety will bring on all sorts of wonderful things! I thought I had finally overcome fear, but NOOOOO! There it was again. The intense fear returned. I started to cry and, in the privacy of my bedroom, said, "Please God, take me home, I'm really tired of this."

That night I had a dream. Spirit said, **"You've had every fear there is so that you can help people."** Well, thanks a lot! It wasn't much consolation then, but later, when I was working as a healer and had conquered the worst of it, I understood. It really was true. There never has been anyone that I didn't understand, thanks to of all of my own painful years filled with fear. After that dream, I would always know that when the anxiety returned, the fear was rearing its ugly head again. I would affirm how patient I was—calm, quiet, and at peace.

To Become Quiet and Peaceful – Breathe.

Do a breathing exercise. Breathe in deeply to the count of eight, hold your breath to the count of four, and then exhale out to the count of eight, hold yourself empty to the count of four, and start the process again. Keep doing it until you let go of the fear. The mind can only concentrate on one thing at a time. By doing the breathing exercise, you will eventually get rid of the fear and relax. It works wonders for getting the mind out of a rut.

Making the sound "OM" creates the same magic. It gives your mind a new focus. This exercise, plus visualizations, will help you to quiet down and straighten out your life.

My first step out of the rut was Concept Therapy. It taught that our thoughts give form to the energy that eventually manifests on the physical level. In other words, everything begins with an idea. To change what manifests around you, change your ideas. It sounds simple but is not always so easy to do. Ideas that we focus on and give lots of energy to become belief systems or concepts. They then move to the emotional level, where they affect us as feelings. Lastly, they manifest as our reality on the physical level. Some of these ideas are buried deeply in our subconscious minds and manifest in strange, ugly little ways, like the "untouchable." Some of them, on the other hand, bring us joy and the good things in life. I try to be very conscious of my thoughts and belief systems. My behavior and emotional reactions to the people around me will show me what my beliefs are.

Not only do we see ourselves in others—the duality—but we find our belief systems in some of the strangest places. I was traveling in Hawaii when I heard a tour guide say something about missionaries. I felt my back prickle and I heard myself say, "Missionaries should be boiled in oil!" I thought to myself, "You seem to have a bit of a problem here. You must have been one of the worst of them."

Once, years ago, I saw the NOW. Everything was happening at the same time, as the bowl described in Chapter 2. The past was on my left, the present was in front of me, and the future was on my right. It really frightened me, as I didn't know where I belonged in all of it.

I also did a lot of regression therapy before I started doing Reiki. In a regression, I would focus on a problem that I was having and ask Spirit to show me the cause of the difficulty. Often I would then see a vision of whatever caused the problem. Once I understood the source, I could then address it intelligently, and heal the issue.

In Egypt, I was walking through one of the temples and again I heard a guide say that the Coptics had defaced the hieroglyphics on the walls. Having great reverence for all things Egyptian, I immediately became angry about it. I then saw a vision of how humanity had overlaid one religion with another for eons of time. Maybe it's a constant process until we recognize that we are all one—all races and all religions. That certainly would bring peace to the world. Wouldn't it?

It wasn't until I read the Seth material that I became consciously aware of the concept that you create your own reality. I began to understand the depth of the teaching. Consciousness and energy create the nature of reality. You create your own reality. *Makia*—energy flows where attention goes. All are just different ways of saying the same thing. It seems so much easier to sit back and blame everything and everyone, but it really is a lot more painful than taking responsibility for your life. Taking responsibility for your creations is the first step to knowing that you are one with God.

If you don't like what you've created, you can change it. Looking for someone else to free you keeps you stuck. Co-dependence comes on many levels—Prince Charming, Snow White, or people coming from outer space to rescue you. A slave is a person who is waiting for someone else to come and free him or her. Free yourself. With it comes confidence, self-esteem, and empowerment.

With that knowledge under my belt, I began to tackle the agoraphobia. The first step was to put all my faith in the God within me. At that time, I was in this mess held together by anger, resentment, good intentions, and the sheer force of will. I learned about affirmations, that is, affirming what I wanted to be true in my life. I would repeat a thought over and over again, the exact opposite of what was *really* happening or true at the time in my life, until I finally believed what I wanted to be true. It is the process of reprogramming your computer. Affirmations enable you to change your ideas and your attitudes.

All these little tricks helped me make it through the night, along with the wonderful affirmation that I learned from The Unity Church: **There is only one presence and one power, God, the Good, Omniscient.** I realized that if I wasn't seeing the good in a situation, then I wasn't seeing God. I could then work on how I perceived a situation, I would start by trying to see the good in it. Then I could see God and the beauty of it.

When we don't like what's happening to us, and it feels frightening or worse than we can deal with, we bury it in our subconscious minds. These buried emotions lie deep within us and act on us unconsciously. They affect our behavior patterns until we are ready to bring those old, unhappy experiences to the conscious level, acknowledge them, and let them go. Examples of this would be the "untouchable" that I buried, or abused people who never wanted to acknowledge that someone they loved could possibly do that to them. Buried emotions can also create diseases, or cause people to grind their teeth all night long rather than talk about what happened to them. Once recognized, the anger and the fear that they have been holding back comes forth and the illness disappears. Repressed energy often results in compulsive behavior.

All of the "-aholic" issues come from not wanting to feel what we feel, or know to be true, so we work frantically, shop, drink, or indulge in coffee, cigarettes, alcohol, or drugs, or keep busy, or watch TV—anything to avoid feeling those feelings! The energy has to go somewhere. It's like air in a plastic bag; if you push down in one place, it comes up in another. People become like tethered balloons. They want to fly, but these buried feelings keep them unhappy and unhealthy, tied to the problem. The emotional body is directly related to the spiritual body. Wanting to change your life begins the process of bringing the buried issues to consciousness.

Look at the most difficult problem in your life. Thank God for it, knowing that in its overcoming, you will gain greatly. Out of fear comes strength, faith, and mastery.

Think of yourself as being a sailboat on the waters of life. A storm can capsize you, or, if you take firm control and use all the strength and focus you have, you can use the strong winds to blow you home even faster.

In my overcoming process, I found an angry person under all that spirituality I professed. Somehow I had gotten the idea that it wasn't "spiritual" to ever say NO, so I didn't. I also never said, "Stop hurting me, or treating me like that." I never said either of those things, or anything else. All I ever said was, "FINE—I'M FINE." This, of course, added to the problem. I was a walking nervous breakdown, and holding on so tightly by repressing it, not expressing how I felt deep down, that I made myself sick. I had to be perfect!

When I first went to teach in Japan, my contact told me that the way to do business with the Japanese was to never put them in a position where they had to say no. It was important to come from intuition and create harmony, to stand back and give them plenty of space. After we all knew each other, we could then discuss business. As she talked, tears rolled down my face. "Finally," I thought. "I get it! I'm a Japanese person trying to live in the United States."

In years past, when someone asked me to do something that I didn't want to do, I remember saying, "Why are you asking me to do that?" In my imagination, I would say to them, "I would never ask you to do that." I didn't know I had the right to say no. Well, Reiki healed that, and I have in turn helped many Japanese people to express and empower themselves with their own healing modality.

I have found in my years of healing how important it is to *feel what you feel.* It isn't a matter of right or wrong. It is what you feel. What you *do* about what you feel is what's important. It is important to express your feelings and, once again, it's how you express them that's important. You do want to express them safely in a way that will not harm you or your relationships.

Because I was afraid to say "No," or anything else for that matter, I never stood up for myself. The way I describe that situation is, "I was so afraid to say anything, I allowed people to knife me to the wall with their criticism, anger, or humiliation. When all appendages were knifed to the wall, I would pull the whole house down on them." It wasn't a particularly healthy way of dealing with my emotions, but it did work.

I saw an article in the newspaper about a woman who was bedridden after hemorrhoid surgery, forced to lie on her abdomen. She became infuriated at her husband for filling a cooler with beer to spend Sunday afternoon fishing with his friends. When he returned six hours later, she shot and killed him when he came in the door. She got rid of that pain in the butt! The body will express what our mouths dare not say. Again, effective, but there are better ways to release that pent-up rage.

My feelings were always hurt. I expected the whole world to know how to treat me. If they really loved me, they would know. What a set-up!! It's a set-up for failure. How many of you do that? Be honest! Most people are not mind-readers. You have to tell people how you feel and what will make you happy and teach them how to treat you. Even then, there are times that you will have to negotiate and temper what you say. When everything is out in the open, you can talk about it instead of nursing wounds inside that will make you sick if you hold on to them for a long time.

Because I had the belief that it wasn't spiritual to say no, I never did. If someone asked me to do something, I always said yes whether I wanted to or not. Believe me, if you say yes and you really mean no, you will create a lot of havoc in your body. Your subconscious is saying no while your conscious mind is saying yes. You are a house divided. That pull within you is a tug of war creating anxiety and duality within you. It took me years to learn to speak up and say no rather than being resentful.

I met a yogi around that time who told me that I was holding a lot of hostility in my chest. That was the understatement of the year. I never talked about how I felt. As I said before, if asked how I was, my response was " FINE!" and if anyone asked me what the problem was, my answer was, "NOTHING!" Not a great communicator in those days. He told me that I needed to release all that hostility, to turn on some music, and let my body shake it out.

The first time I did the shake-out exercise, I went into my bedroom and stated my intention of shaking out that hostility. I wasn't feeling it at the time, at least no more than usual. I turned on my belly dance music as loud as I could and let her rip! I started flapping my arms like a chicken and making a few weird noises. I began to feel very tribal and aware of deep feelings.

I have found that if you shake out your emotions until your body lets go and relaxes completely the first time, after that you can very easily shake out any emotion quickly in the bathroom or wherever, if you have to give a speech, have an interview, or have difficulty at work.

It only takes a minute. Shaking out completely and forgiving is called "dumping the cosmic garbage can." It's a good thing to do periodically. Then you don't let emotions build up.

Today there is all sorts of drumming music in the stores that is much more appropriate for shaking out, but back in the seventies, my belly dance music was the best I knew of, and it worked.

It came to me that perhaps when we were tribal people and lived close to the earth, we knew what to do with our emotions. Maybe war dances were done to release warring feelings, as well as to rev people up to prepare them for war. I shook, kicked, made strange sounds, and hit the air for about two hours. All of a sudden, my body let go. I started to cry and heard myself say, "I'm afraid to love." That came as a big shock! I thought I was the most loving being on two feet. How could I, wonderful me, not be loving? After all, I never said no to anyone and never told anyone how I felt.

I was never angry, so how could I not be loving? It took me years to learn that acting out of fear was not love. It took me what seemed like eons to learn how to change my fears to love.

Slowly I realized that I wasn't loving—I was really resentful, because I didn't set boundaries for myself. People would stay at my house forever. I never could throw them out. Now I've learned to express myself with words like, "Say good-night, Chris," or whoever it was. Humor gets you a long way.

I had to buy a tape on Assertiveness Training to be able to do it. On that tape, they said that you had to say no five times before someone heard you. I tried it out and it was true. Then I had so much fun saying no that I would do it all the time. It felt powerful for me after being such a wimp. It was fun! I could actually stop people. After a few times, I didn't have to prove anything any more, and I found some polite ways to say no, such as, "That doesn't work for me."

Shortly thereafter, I had ordered a product from a student of mine, and he wanted to deliver it at dinnertime. Previously I would have talked to him forever while my dinner burned. This time I told him that he could deliver it then if I could just hand him a check, but he would have to leave because it was our dinnertime. He agreed readily. It was easy.

I was amazed! I found that when I began to set boundaries, I felt safe and protected. The world was not such a scary place and I wasn't so angry or such a victim.

A girlfriend of mine, who was well-meaning but controlling, would come over all the time and bring me vitamins I had not asked her to buy for me. I would thank her and offer to pay her for them. After a while that got tiresome and expensive. I decided that I needed to stop it. The next time she brought them to me, I thanked her profusely but did not offer to pay her. That stopped the unsolicited purchases immediately. Today, I wouldn't have difficulty telling her that I didn't want the friggin' vitamins, but did appreciate her thoughtfulness. In those days, though, I couldn't say much of anything to anyone.

Anger can be a great motivation to get things done, when we use it properly. Most people are afraid of their anger because they express it destructively. They generally become like walking volcanoes, as I did, or like the eighty-four-year-old woman in a wheelchair I read about who killed her husband with a bedpan because he had taunted her for forty years about the affair he was having. They repress emotions, stuffing it all down until they can't take it any longer. Often they then dump their anger on some poor, unsuspecting individual who is safe—generally not even the right person to change the situation.

EXERCISES

Examine the patterns in your life. Are you happy with them, or are you still acting out someone else's desires for you? Are they Mom and Dad all over again?

I have come a long way from the person who was afraid to tell the clerk she didn't want the rotten cucumber at the grocery store—just by setting my own boundaries and expressing how I feel.

More illnesses are caused by repressed anger and negative emotions than all the food, cigarettes, or germs, in the world. It's important to release the bottled-up emotions in safe ways: by screaming, running, beating pillows, shaking out, writing, or any other technique that works for you, without harming yourself or others. Do them all alone and allow plenty of time to do them. Finding proper channels for the release of pent-up emotions will cut down greatly on illness and abuse.

Once I shook out all that "stuff," I began to verbalize all of the billions of things I had never voiced before such as, "If you want me to contribute to your cause, please ask me politely rather than telling me what my share is," or "If you want this relationship to last, then please speak to me politely rather than yelling, even if I have made a mistake or a million or them."

Once I began to stand up for myself, I wasn't nearly as hostile or frightened as I had been. When I began to create boundaries and take care of myself, I felt protected. I wasn't so defensive. I was even becoming easier to be around. I realized that I was being very unfair to people by never telling them what disturbed me. How could anyone ever get along with me, since I didn't tell them the truth?

I thought if they loved me, they should know how I felt. "Fine" no longer cut it. I stopped "shoulding" on everybody and made a big effort to communicate and tell the truth. I believe that people can resolve anything if they are willing and have the courage to say what they want to say and do it with love.

The Great Shake-Down!

Turn on some music and let your body shake out the fear, pain, anger, anxiety, jealousy, or whatever you're feeling. Keep going until your body completely lets go. Like an earthquake, shake it long enough 'til that old stuff just breaks away. Your body might want to start making noises—kick or punch the air. Allow your body to do whatever it needs to do in order to let go and relax. **Do Not Criticize Your Body!** Your body will never lie to you about what it's feeling and where it's storing emotions. Your mind, however, can screw you over six ways to Christmas and rationalize anything. **Trust your body!** It knows what it needs to heal itself! It will tell you what emotions it's holding. Then you will know what ideas need to be changed. Remember, it starts first in the mind, then moves to the emotional body, and lastly manifests in the physical body.

You will find after you have released all that tremendous energy, it will be far easier to confront situations in your life calmly and logically. You will be able to lovingly verbalize your feelings without accusation. Once you do this exercise until your body completely relaxes, you can easily release anything in minutes, just by shaking it out. If I have to give a speech and am afraid, I have been able to run into the ladies room and shake out fear in a few seconds. I can then walk on stage and be calm and have a good time.

Shake out or write out how you feel. Just allow your feelings to come up. Start with what you know to be true, and keep writing, allowing your subconscious to supply the buried feelings.

Start with a heading such as I hate _____. (Don't rationalize, sweetie! We all know how "spiritual" you are. Allow those painful feelings to come out.)

- I hate _____ because _____
- I'm angry at _____ because_____
- I'm afraid of _____ (person) because _____
- I'm afraid of failure because_____
- I'm afraid of the unknown because _____
- I'm afraid of love because _____
- I'm afraid of _____

Make up your own. Start writing what you know and let the rest of it come up. If you need to talk to someone and you are frightened or angry, shake out or write out all that emotion first. Then you will be able to speak lovingly and rationally to them.

One time our daughter was in school and working two jobs. She had met a young man and suddenly I had a feeling that she wasn't in school that day. I called the school to find out if she was there and said that I was just checking up on my investment. They informed me that they hadn't seen her for six weeks. My blood started to boil. The longer I had to wait for her to come home, the angrier I got. I was waiting for her so I could throw her out. When she finally came home, I was ready to blow my top. She walked in and said, "Hi, Mom." She was as cheery as could be.

I said, "Excuse me a minute," and went into my room and shook out all of that volcanic energy that was ready to devastate her and everything around. Instead of just screaming my head off to expend the energy and maybe or maybe not touching on the issue, I could then very quietly and lovingly state that she was welcome to live her life as she chose, but if she wanted to stay in our house, she had to be in school to learn a profession, and then get a job. (I had learned that she had also quit the two jobs she had.) I gave her three weeks to do it or find another place to live. She said, "I agree with you," and was back on track within a week.

It could have been very explosive had I not done the "Great Shake-Down" first. I would have screamed and yelled to expend the energy, probably have demeaned her character, and maybe or maybe not even have touched on the issue. This time I nipped it in the bud. It was easy with very positive communication between us. Our relationship was intact. I believe that almost anything can be resolved if it is communicated in a loving way. Most often it's not what you say but the way you say it that creates the difficulty.

Shaking out, doing yoga, or doing any exercise helps to quiet you and prepare for meditation.

How to Meditate

Do it twenty to thirty minutes per day . . . forever.

Meditation is invaluable for a number of reasons. It helps you relax. When you are relaxed, your natural juices can flow, which makes you healthier. You can program your life in a more meaningful way with hypnosis or with visualization. That makes you happier. Or you can use meditation to discover all of the hidden treasures within you, and that helps immeasurably. Sit or lie down in a comfortable place. Keep your back straight. If you're snoring, that's not meditation!

For pure relaxation, close your eyes and see yourself in your own perfect place in nature, or whatever turns you on. You can be in the mountains where you can see forever, next to a beautiful waterfall, on the beach, in the desert, or wherever you feel best. Feel yourself being nurtured by the purity of your surroundings, and healed by the gentle breezes and the beauty there. Breathe in the revitalizing energy of nature and relax completely.

You can just close your eyes, place yourself in God's loving hands, ask for guidance, and see what happens. Even if you think that nothing is happening, something is. You will feel better. Sometimes I will ask a question and wait for an answer.

In the beginning, try to do this daily and at the same time of day. Disregard any mental conversation about what you're going to fix for dinner, the clothes that need to be picked up at the cleaners, the work that needs to be done, and so on. Gently turn your mind to the God within you. Breathe regularly and allow whatever happens to you to happen. You can focus on your breath if you wish. You can breathe in The White Light of Protection and breathe away any fears, discomfort, or the cares of the day. When I first started, I found that nothing seemed to happen at all for quite a few weeks. And then suddenly, I started seeing visions while ironing or cleaning out the refrigerator.

After that, I began to see and hear messages in meditation. You always receive the fruits of meditation, even if you don't see or hear anything at all during the process. Stress will slowly disappear, your trust level will be enhanced, and your health will improve. You do not need to do anything more than this. However, you can make your meditations more elaborate by visualizing quiet scenes or calling forth a guide to bring you a message. You can ask questions of the guide if you choose. See yourself in nature or in a place where you can relax. Be patient with yourself. You will receive all that is right for you.

Becoming quiet and turning your mind to God opens the door to a new consciousness and the sanctuary. It enhances your psychic ability and increases your intuition. Anything can happen! Remember the bowl. All power is within and there are no limits.

I once saw this in a meditation: When you start learning a new activity, think of yourself as a little flower coming up through the earth from a seed. The stem is so fragile. Think of all the energy it takes for the little flower to push through the earth. Your lack of patience and self-criticism are like picking up your foot with a heavy boot on and crushing that tiny flower, telling it it's not growing fast enough, it's the wrong color, or it's not pretty enough. It sounds terrible, doesn't it? Many people do that to themselves. It is what keeps them tight in their container (ego) rather that opening to the glories of creation and the beauty of their soul. You would never do that to a little flower. Do you do it to yourself in your thoughts, with your fear and doubt, while learning new techniques or practicing old ones?

MEDITATION EXERCISE

See a little flower in your mind's eye, the little flower that you are. Tell it you love it. Nurture it. Talk to it lovingly and encourage its growth. Do this daily . . . forever.

You might want to see a luminous being who heals you, fills you with love, and gives you the guidance you need for your life at the moment. You can do this whenever you wish. These methods access the deeper mind.

In the beginning of my spiritual quest, I went to a psychic who told me to meditate with Tarot cards. The Tarot cards are a deck of seventy-eight cards designed to teach universal wisdom and human behavior through symbolism. They are pictorial representations of the principles, or laws, of life. They can also be used for divination. At that time, I was so new to metaphysics that I didn't know what either meditation or Tarot cards were. I bought a deck and sat down daily and just looked at the cards. I immediately recognized the tenth card, which was the Wheel of Fortune. It was the depiction of my dream, except it wasn't as grim—no one was tied to the wheel. I would pick one card a day to focus on. Slowly I began to get ideas about the cards. I would write down what I received or "heard." Hearing can be different in meditation. Sometimes it will be an actual voice; other times it's a feeling of hearing a word or a message. Seeing can be the same. Sometimes I actually see things. Often I feel the presence of a form.

For a long time, I just sat there and nothing happened. Then I began to see and hear things. Eventually I began to see and hear whole events acted out for me, which became a series of children's stories. All the while, I thought that I wasn't doing meditation correctly, at least not "according to the books." When I finally took a meditation class, I said, "Oh, this is meditation. I've been doing this for years!" Always trust that what you are receiving is right for you—no matter what the books say or anyone else tells you. Never doubt the Spirit within you!

Keep doing meditation even though it may seem like nothing is happening. Eventually it will become a valuable tool. It brings relaxation, lowers your blood pressure, and puts you in touch with the God within you, whether you see or hear anything or not.

After a while, I stopped using all the techniques to make meditation happen. I would just close my eyes and go what I call "out." I believe scientifically one would call that going to a deeper level. Alpha, Beta, Gamma, Delta, Omega, Psi, Fee, Fi, Fo, Fum, or whatever they call it. I'm not good on the terminology or the Greek alphabet either, for that matter. Some call it the void, or the unknown. I call it God.

Eventually I got to the place where I could sit down, ask a question, and wait for the answer to come, either in voice, visual, or feeling form. It was great! Believe me, once you get involved in the deeper mind, it's better than the movies. Nothing can compare!

When you get in touch with the inner guidance, the guide, or your God, whatever you wish to call it, and follow it, your life begins to turn around. You are never alone, fears begin to melt away, and healing comes. Guidance from within is always loving and always right for all concerned when you follow it. It may not be what your ego wants to see or hear, but it's always right for your soul. It's a wonderful way to develop confidence and a sense of self-worth. It makes you comfortable in your container and opens you to the greater Universe around you, so that you can move out of your ego to allow your soul to come forth. The soul is that part of you that knows it is one with its Source. Meditating is the first step to recovery and healing.

As I practiced meditation, my horrible feeling of loneliness disappeared, and I began to feel loved and safe in the world. I remember one time early in my marriage when my feelings were hurt about something. I was feeling unloved, asking God to help me to feel His/Her love so deep within me that I didn't have to look for it from somebody else. Slowly I began to feel it. It wasn't until I found meditation and the inner guidance that my feelings of being alone disappeared.

A Course in Miracles states that there is nothing but God. If we are seeing anything other than love, it is merely an illusion and a reflection of our own inner being. It also says that all relationships are anger relationships designed to make the other person feel guilty. We feel angry because we are not getting the love we want from the other person, so we try to make them feel guilty to get them to love us. When we read this in class one night, I was all excited about it and wanted my husband to listen to what I had just read. He wasn't interested.

I tried every which way to get him to listen or read it for himself. He told me to do it with my girlfriends. I got angry, and then I tried to manipulate him and make him feel guilty. The *Course* was right! I did exactly what it said! Eventually, I could laugh at myself. It is powerful information and the truth. We will never receive from another the love that we want because they can't give it to us. Only God can give us the love that we want. Everything else is insufficient and leaves us unfulfilled. That is why meditation is so important. It enables us to feel the love that is deep within us and helps us to remember who we really are.

The more you turn your life over to the God within you and ask for divine guidance, the happier, healthier, and more peaceful you become. Spirit will always lead you to what is best for all concerned. You can always ask for a guide or an angel to guide you while you are in your perfect place in nature. Sometimes you can see these guides. Some people only feel their presence. Ask your question or ask for healing and wait for the response. Ask and ye shall receive. Trust that you will receive. Be quiet and wait for the answer. It always comes. It may not always be the way we expect it to arrive. Often it arrives in the meditation. But the answer can also come from a phone call, a letter, or something that you read in the paper or see on television. A feeling will run through you and you will know that it is your answer sent directly from Heaven to you. Sometimes God works in mysterious ways.

chapter 4

If You Can Conceive It, You Can Achieve It!

Affirmations and Creative Visualization

C reative visualization works in two ways. We set up exercises to allow buried feelings to surface, and through visualization, we can create what we want to manifest. The subconscious mind does not know the difference between imagination and reality. It will create what you image or imagine to be true. It will create what you are focusing on. Remember my missed 10:05 flight. When you are imaging, you are eliminating the conscious mind and speaking directly to the subconscious.

Examples: During the years of my agoraphobia, to lessen the problem, I would spend a great deal of time visualizing that I had already been to a place long before I actually went to the event. I would see myself talking to a friend in my mind's eye, saying how wonderful it was that I had gone wherever it was, had a lovely time, and was **calm, quiet, and at peace.**

Eventually I would begin to calm down. Think of your mind as a scale with one cup for the negative energy and another cup for the positive energy. Have you been filling that negative cup with your worry or fear for years? If so, now you have to fill the cup on the positive side with equal amounts of energy to neutralize the negative energy, so it all just IS, neither positive nor negative, and the scales are balanced. Generally, it takes many positive affirmations to neutralize the negative in your life.

Affirmations are sentences such as, "There's nobody here but God," which you repeat as often as you need until it takes hold. What you are doing is filling the positive cup on the scale. **Affirm what you want to become true for you,** the exact opposite of what is manifesting for you at that time. When we have equalized the energy in the cups on the scale, they no longer sway positive or negative—good nor bad—the energy is neutralized and everything just IS. The duality is gone. Then we can act freely and positively, without emotion, free of stress.

Another example: As a child, I would go down to the basement, frightened all the while that the boogeyman or whatever lived down there would grab me. I was always an imaginative child and could create a great case of the Heebie-Jeebies! I did such a good job that it finally happened. Fear adds enormous feeling and energy to the image so that it magnetizes the experience right to us. In the words of Job, "The thing that I fear the most has come upon me." A friend grabbed me down there in the dark basement just as I imagined it would happen. He thought it was hysterically funny, but I collapsed onto the floor in terror.

From then on, I would only go down to the basement with another person or try to get someone else to go down there to get what I wanted. As an adult, my family finally caught on and no one would go down to the basement for me.

I had to start facing the fear and getting over it. Every time I went down to the basement, I would wrap myself in the White Light of God. Think of the Light as that of a diamond or fireworks, Light being the first Creation of God, as it states in the Bible. "In the beginning the Earth was without form and void. The Spirit of God moved over the face of the living waters and God said, 'Let there be light' and there was light." This Light contains the protective power and knowledge of the Universe. I would repeat constantly while I was down there, "There's nobody here but God," which meant to me that I was safe and protected, and there was nothing to fear.

Finally, one day, I realized that I wasn't going through all those elaborate machinations just to get a box of peas from the freezer. I could go down to the basement without fear. There actually was nothing there but God. I could act spontaneously without fear. I never again went down to the basement or anywhere else feeling afraid that the boogeyman was lurking there, waiting to jump out and grab me. When the fear was released, I never thought of it again. I had created a new reality. The basement was now safe. Once I was able to overcome my greatest fear, the world became a friendlier place.

How to Kick The Habit

The two signs on the ancient Greek temples were ***Know Thyself*** and ***Nothing in Excess***. If you have looked at yourself and your behavior and found yourself wanting, there are a number of ways to change your behavior, but all of them start with a decision. The decision has to be made that the old way of looking to someone else to fill that void or emptiness within you isn't working and you are ready to look for alternatives. If you continue with the old lottery system—maybe the next one will be the winner—you are doomed. You didn't get any satisfaction there before, and you won't ever unless you change the premise. Make the decision to love yourself enough to give yourself what you want and acknowledge that you are worthy of having a joyous life. If you hate yourself for doing something, stop doing it! If you constantly criticize yourself, stop it!

Case in point: I loved to smoke! I was a very heavy cigarette smoker for years. That was before they called it an addiction. Even though I loved to smoke and didn't have any physical problems because of it, I hated myself because I wasn't in control. Cigarettes controlled me. I tried to quit smoking about five times, and, at one point in time, I had quit for good, or so I thought. But then I had a dream that said, "When you're on the top of one mountain, you're at the bottom of another." Well, thanks a lot!!! That scared the bejesus out of me. Quitting was horrible enough! What was it going to be after that??? I went back to smoking for another five years.

I finally decided that I would never love myself until I quit smoking for good. This time I bought a hypnosis tape. It was entitled *Stop Smoking* by Dick Sutphen. Often the most difficult problems bring the greatest gifts. Now it was really time to quit. I was then faced with all of my fears. I didn't think that I could live and not smoke. (That was in 1979, so I obviously lived through it.) The plan of the tape package was to count how many cigarettes you smoked, to discover how many a day you needed to eliminate in order to be at zero by the end of a two-week period, and then listen to the enclosed tape daily.

The instruction on the tape was to see yourself in your imagination talking to a friend, telling them how wonderful you feel because you are a nonsmoker, and to make it as real as possible. When I started the process, I couldn't even close my eyes and see myself without a cigarette. On the tape, it says to imagine that someone walks up to you and offers you a cigarette, and again you reply that you are a nonsmoker. I did the tape twice a day for two weeks because I thought that I was the worst case scenario. Then it was D-day!

It really wasn't as hard to quit as it had been before. I still had to use my will power, but it wasn't as painful as it had been in the past. Visualization increases will power. I have discovered a number of things since then. For those of you who smoke, you are creating a smokescreen, and it's a way to express your buried anger. Think of it—you are fuming. Find other ways to express your anger and it will be much easier to quit the habit. Try any of the exercises I've mentioned before.

There's a lot of rebellion in smoking. I found that out when I told my mother that I had quit smoking before and didn't. I was smoking behind the garage to hide from her like a little kid. One of my sons caught me in the act. Busted!!! I realized what a terrible example I was setting. When I faced my fears and smoked in front of her, it empowered me in an odd way. I was then free to quit on my own. That was teenager behavior, I admit.

From the very beginning of this new venture, I kept a pack of cigarettes nearby and would say to myself a number of times a day, "I can smoke if I want to, but I choose not to." Making it my choice empowered me and helped me to love myself. I have found also that when I quit worrying about what someone else thinks about me, it is very freeing! I have had a number of bouts with that subject.

I was on my third day of not smoking when a friend, who had quit smoking five years prior to that, came over for a spaghetti dinner. I remember it like it was yesterday. After dinner, my husband, Ray, lit a cigarette. My friend, who had quit five years prior to that, said, "Oh, God, that looks good!" You can just imagine what went through me. I was still running around smelling ashtrays, but not smoking! But I sure wanted to. Desire ran rampant through me. Every part of my being craved a cigarette. But I recognized the problem. In the past, after quitting a few days, I would wonder if I still wanted to smoke. So, I would kid myself and just try one. "That tastes awful. I'll just have to try another." And pretty soon I was back at it. This time, I realized that allowing myself to think that it looked good and that I wanted to smoke was out of the question. Those thoughts made my body go berserk. If I affirmed that I chose not to smoke, my cravings would calm down. Everything starts first in the mind, then manifests on the emotional level, and lastly in the physical body. Focus on what you want to create. Focus on the solution, not the problem.

That visualization technique is the best and the easiest that I know of to create anything in your life that you want. A while after that, we went through a severe financial crisis. I would see myself in my imagination talking to my favorite saleslady in the dress shop where I used to be able to buy my clothes, telling her how wonderful it was that we had plenty of money to pay our bills. In time, money started to flow, and we had just enough money to pay the bills, but nothing left over. I started again, this time telling her how wonderful it was that we had plenty of money to pay the bills and plenty left over for fun. Money began to flow into our lives. Since then, I had a dream that told me that it takes two weeks for something new to manifest.

It is important to keep your focus on what you want to manifest. Don't move back into "poor little me"—"I don't have any money; I can't help it; I can't do this; it's too hard; it doesn't work for me; I'm sick; or nobody loves me. Think of it like a football field. You have a goal at either end. One goal is to quit smoking, lose weight, or whatever you are creating. The other goal is to smoke, gobble goodies, etc. Don't jump back and forth between the two. That creates tension. You must focus on one goal, otherwise you become like a football player running back and forth across the fifty-yard line. This creates enormous tension while you play tug of war with yourself. It makes you a house divided, which we all know cannot stand. For sure you won't be able to stand it!! Make the decision and stay with it. It works, and it is far easier than you think it will be. Visualize it. Do it! Just do it!!

When you are doing this visualization, you are actually doing three things: affirming what you want to be true, programming your subconscious mind, and trusting in the Spirit within you to bring you what is right for you—and it does.

I have used visualization in the past to bring peace and relaxation, money, to lose weight, and in all sorts of other ways. If I have to go someplace and I'm nervous about it, I will see it all going easily and well. Occasionally, I will recognize that I'm complaining about my weight or something else and not using the visualization. Then I ask myself why I want the extra weight or whatever it is that I'm complaining about. If I really don't want it, I change it. That's true for everyone.

When I find myself doubting, I remember that consciousness and energy create reality. Doubting yourself is one of the worst things you can do. If you stay focused on what you want, you will create it. Cause and effect always work. For every action, there's an opposite and equal reaction. Give it plenty of time to manifest. If it isn't working for you, check out your hidden agenda. Ask Spirit to help you to see what's in the way. Are you too afraid to be successful? Are you afraid to fail? Afraid to share your life with a partner? Afraid of being hurt? Examine your true feelings.

I remember one time, when I was screaming the most about not having any money, I recognized that not having money gave me an excuse that people would accept. At that time in my life, I was pretty much too afraid to do most things. "I can't afford it" is a sentence that nobody debates.

There are only three excuses that people don't argue with—I can't afford it, I'm sick, and I have to work. The realization that deep down I really didn't want money rocked my solar system. I set to work releasing my fears of leaving my comfort zone. I would practice going out and eating in new and interesting restaurants. I armed myself with my visualizations and affirmations until I wasn't frightened anymore. Once I wasn't frightened anymore, the world was my oyster. I was open for adventure, no longer needing an excuse to stay home. It opened the door for prosperity.

Quitting smoking was one of the most difficult things I ever had to do, but I received so much from it. Once I quit, I had to deal with the emotions behind it. If you smoke, use drugs, or eat or drink too much, this technique works, but you have to really work at it. Make your intention to quit, then start visualizing. When you overcome a habit or change a behavior that makes you hate yourself, it brings enormous self-esteem, and really empowers you. Whatever it is that you do that makes you feel guilty (and consequently, defensive) it's worth the time and the effort to conquer it. Nobody can ever take that away from you.

I also learned about the mind-body connection. When I said that I really wanted to smoke, the urge was quite powerful, and I really had to fight it. But when I said that I chose not to smoke, it was easier. I continued to do the visualization for a while because I would have a dream about a lit cigarette in an ashtray and feared that I had started smoking again. Eventually it all subsided. The trauma was over. I learned that I could do things and just not smoke. Life was back to normal, and I was left with the greatest gift—visualization.

I realized after using this method that I could use it to create anything I wanted. That idea terrified me. Today I can see that I didn't have the self-esteem to feel worthy enough to give myself anything I wanted. At that time, I just ran away from the idea, but quitting smoking empowered me, and I was on the road to feeling worthy. It took a lot of years of healing to reach the point where I could feel worthy of receiving all the good things in life. The untouchable was deeply buried in me.

There's a wonderful story about a woman who went to visit the famous sculptor Rodin. She admired his work immensely and asked him how he accomplished his great works in marble. He responded by saying, "It's very simple, Madam. I just knock off what I don't want!" You, too, are creating a masterpiece—you. Every time you knock off a chunk of what you don't want, you become more harmonious and beautiful, and after a while, you actually will like everything that you see in the mirror. So whatever it is that you are doing that you don't like, KNOCK IT OFF!!

Affirmations are wonderful ways to change your attitudes. Attitude is everything! I woke up one morning with this sentence: I LOVE AND APPRECIATE MY BEAUTIFUL FACE AND BREASTS. I now repeat it so often that my attitude toward my body is changing. I recently realized that my body was part of Earth, and if I could love my body, I could help heal the Earth, as well. So do your part for Mother Earth. Love and appreciate your beautiful body. Think of what it does for you. It allows you to hug a tree, hold a loved one, and manifest here on Earth.

My friend Jeremy used to teach an affirmation class. He had a woman in his class who was the epitome of what every woman wants to be. She was beautiful and had a lovely body. He told me how surprised everyone in the class was because she didn't see herself that way and had the same complaints as the rest of the class about her looks. It's universal. Most women, maybe men, too, are dissatisfied with how they look, so affirmations are really important. Affirm your inner beauty, and do something about the outside if you don't like it. Remember the bowl. Remember who you really are, created in the image of God.

One of my favorite affirmations is: I CAN DO THIS WITH EASE AND WITH GRACE. This affirmation came to me one Christmas when we had been out of town and I was really behind in the shopping and in a panic. The more I repeated the phrase, the more relaxed I became. I opened my gift closet and found a lot of things that I forgot I had already stashed away. Everything flowed so easily. It was amazing. It was the nicest Christmas ever.

I CHOOSE JOY INSTEAD OF PAIN is another one of my all-time favorites. I broke my little toe one time before I was leaving for New York where I would be walking for days, and then going on to Europe for two weeks of more walking. I opened the book *A Course in Miracles* for help and turned to the lesson titled "I Choose Joy Instead of Pain." I repeated the affirmation every time my toe started to hurt, and I was fine. The pain would go away. It worked. Sometimes I change it to I CHOOSE JOY INSTEAD OF FEAR if I'm afraid of something. For a long time, I was afraid all the time. I would repeat I AM CALM, QUIET, AND AT PEACE. NOTHING CAN DISTURB THE CALM PEACE OF MY SOUL about a thousand times a day.

Back then, my self-esteem would have to climb three feet to come up to low. I would buy a new outfit to look what I considered fabulous in order to make it through any event to just feel good enough. I compared myself to everyone and always came up wanting. I read, I studied, meditated, and did affirmations and visualizations a billion times. Everything helped. Just as I was improving, we went through the financial crisis I mentioned earlier, and I couldn't buy a new outfit to make it through the night anymore. I didn't think that anyone would want to be with me because we had no money. I didn't think that I had anything to give. That's when I found Reiki. Healing myself and others helped enormously. Through that struggle, I learned self-worth.

I was asked to speak at a women's weekend at The American Club, a five-star resort that is part of the Kohler Company in Kohler, Wisconsin—yes, the bathroom people. My husband Ray was going to be doing a talk on creativity there, as well. We had traded them our services for their renewal package, which consisted of a massage, facial, and manicure. Because I was going to be doing healings in my room, they gave us a room with a hot tub, steam shower, and all the amenities. The deluxe rooms were the only rooms big enough to hold a massage table. I was ecstatic! I did a talk on Reiki the first day and all went well. The second day we spent in the spa. It was glorious! Ray did his class that evening.

Later that night, I went to my suitcase to take out my purple suit that I had planned to wear the next morning when I did the closing talk. The purple skirt was not there! I FREAKED OUT! Ray very sweetly offered to drive home to get the skirt for me, a two-hour round trip. It didn't feel right to make him do that. I went into the hot tub and asked Ray to leave me alone. I entered into a black hole and felt as though I was in a whirlpool spiraling downward. I knew that sending Ray home was going back into the old fear of not being good enough. I prayed for Spirit to help me. The message I received was: **IT'S NOT WHAT YOU WEAR THAT'S IMPORTANT. IT'S NOT WHAT YOU DO THAT'S IMPORTANT, BUT IT IS WHAT YOU ARE THAT'S IMPORTANT. YOU ARE A DIVINE BEING. NOTHING ELSE MATTERS**.

Once again, the bowl was brought to my mind. I climbed out of the hot tub like a prune. I decided on a pair of white pants to go with the purple jacket. The next morning I shared my plight and the message with the women. We all got a good laugh out of it. The message was important for all of us.

Creating affirmations is a simple procedure. Examine your life and see what needs to be changed. What do you see in others around you? What are you having difficulties with? Start saying the opposite of what is true at the time. What are you afraid of? You can change it.

When I was first married, I was afraid of my husband, for no reason other than that I was afraid of everyone and everything else then, so why not him, too. I would mumble under my breath, "I trust you" all the time, and one day I did.

About ten years ago, we moved into a bigger house. I was always forgetting where I left my purse or shoes, and it required a lot more work. I began to feel like a little rat on a wheel. I had no time to do what I wanted. I realized that I was always saying, "I don't have any time." Of course, it became the truth. That was my mantra, even though I didn't want it. The minute I came to my senses and changed it to, "I have plenty of time to do all that I need to do," I had so much extra time I didn't know what to do with it. For a while, I kept thinking that I had forgotten to do something.

Ideas that we hold and propound become belief systems. Belief systems create our attitudes, which in turn create our reality. This was demonstrated clearly to me when I had two women in a class in California. Both of them had the very same background. Their mothers were cleaning ladies and both of them accompanied their mothers upon occasion. One of them decided that everyone had dirty houses and everyone was the same. She went on to have a happy life. The other decided that her family wasn't as good as everyone else because her mother was cleaning up for the rich people. She had low self-esteem and went on to be unhappy. It was the same exact experience, but different conclusions.

You can change anything. Ask to see it in a new way. Start saying the opposite of what you have been saying and that will change your mind. Change your mind and you change your attitude. Change your attitude and you change your life. Try it—you'll like it! Remember the Reiki class.

See yourself talking to a friend in your imagination about how wonderful your life is, how great you feel about yourself, or whatever you want to manifest. Go for it!

Do it for yourself. Giving yourself what you want is loving yourself. But be careful with this. You can't include anyone else in your visualization, such as, "Herb will love me and want to marry me," "Sally is giving me her fur coat," or "Marie is giving me her job." That is witchcraft, and what goes around comes around. You *can* say, "I have this wonderful partner who wants to marry me, a fabulous fur coat, or great job," and let Spirit fill in the appropriate person and method.

AFFIRMATION AND VISUALIZATION EXERCISE

Make up an affirmation for yourself that will release the past and create for yourself what you want in your life. Remember that consciousness and energy create reality.

See yourself in your mind's eye talking to someone just as though you were there with that person and say to him or her, "Isn't it wonderful that_____." Fill in the blank with whatever you wish to create—I have plenty of money, perfect health, a fabulous relationship, the perfect house, I am safe wherever I go, etc. **Make it very real.** Put as much feeling in it as possible and in time it will manifest. Remember that I had a dream that told me that it takes two weeks to change something.

Putting Visualization to Work

I attended classes at the Meditation Institute for a while. One of the exercises was to create a control room in our imagination and to invite in someone whom we wanted to get to know better. I chose a man in New York with whom I had been having some business dealings. All the while I was having the imaginary conversation with him about our relationship, he was fooling with an amethyst ring I was wearing. My mind kept saying, "This is a crock! This is just my imagination making this all up. It doesn't mean anything. This is stupid!"

Two years later, I went to New York and had the same exact conversation with him. I wouldn't have thought anything of it if he hadn't been sitting there the whole time fooling with my ring.

Believe me, that shocked me! Talk about the Heebie-Jeebies! It let me know how powerful the imagination is. The imagination creates reality even when you don't think it's doing anything. That's why visualization works. Consciousness and energy create reality, so stay with it and keep your visualization going. It works even when you don't think it works. Watch your mind and only create what you want.

Not too long ago, I picked the Angel Card of Patience. The Angel of Patience gave me a beautiful message that made me realize the importance of holding your focus and not doubting yourself or the process of creating your own reality. The illustration on the patience Angel Card shows an angel knitting. In meditation, the angel said to me, "When I sit down to make a sweater, I never once doubt that it's going to be a sweater, even when there are only two stitches on the needle. And by the way, it never looks like a sweater until it's almost all done."

I had been working very hard on my visualization, trying to improve myself, trying to be one with God. I was feeling that I wasn't getting anywhere. That message gave me tremendous inspiration and hope. I feel that it is one of the most important messages I have ever received. HAVE PATIENCE. Practice makes perfect. Remember how long it takes for a flower to grow from a tiny little seed or an angel to make a sweater. Stop and look back at how far you've come. If you're just beginning, take heart, and know that the process works.

If you can conceive it, you can achieve it. Be kind to yourself and keep focused on what you want to manifest in your life.

Creating a New Reality

I had a very interesting experience once at a workshop where we were supposed to lie still and meditate for a whole day. As I began to get into it, I felt a very strong pain in my stomach. I said to God, "What's this about?" and I saw a biblical scene of Solomon's temple being torn down. I felt enormous anger about that. Very soon the pain went away.

Then another pain arrived. When I asked about that one, I saw an elephant and replicas of the Hindu gods on top of the elephant. My anger about the people being so poor and all those golden idols surfaced and that pain went away. Once again, there was another strong pain, and I saw the rush of an ancient Muslim army on horseback. The men were carrying swords screaming, "Infidel!" as they rushed to kill people, and again, the pain subsided. I realized that I had a lot of buried resentment toward almost all organized religions that I needed to forgive. Prior to that experience, I had already seen a few scenes in meditation where I was either quite angry or guilty or both with a few cardinals and bishops in the Catholic religion. I figure that I must have been one of the worst of them, preaching hellfire and damnation. Realizing that religions are just belief systems makes it seem a little silly to have that much animosity, but the whole world is fighting that battle.

It's a shame that there is so much hatred in the world because of what we think God wants. It's just our idea that we project onto God.

Discovering the guilt, the hurts, the jealousies angers, hatreds, and prejudices—

those ideas that we hang onto gleefully and treasure within—can bring up momentary pain when they come to consciousness. But when we become aware of them and release them, we are free of them forever. Once released, we are healed and whole. We become more loving and more receptive to the love that is all around.

A number of years ago, an extraterrestrial being who called himself "Joe" visited me for seventeen days straight. He gave me a series of exercises to do, which became the book *Gods in the Making, or How to Have Fun in the Galaxy,* an earlier book of mine. He gave me new rules to live by starting with Rule 1, which was to *Have Fun,* Rule 2, *Relax,* and then Rule 3, *Relax, Have Fun, and Trust.* He continued on through to Rule 12, *Always Take Your Own Advice.* He talked a lot about the fact that I created what was happening to me, and if I didn't like it, I should create something that I did like. Logical, eh? He continued by saying that we give everything to ourselves, so why wasn't I doing it? Good question! "Joe" is really funny and I adore him! This channeled information helped me to take a good look at myself, raise my self-esteem, and release my seriousness. Because it helped me so much, I published it to help others. As I take steps into unknown territories, I often have to refer back to the information from "Joe."

His lighthearted approach to life was a different perspective from my own very serious striving and struggling to be one with God. I never could remember that I already was God and that there is nothing else. It has taken me years of realization and evolution to allow myself to be loved and feel as though I deserve nurturing and abundance. I can often hear his voice saying to me, "Are you having fun with this yet?" Of course I wasn't!

I was struggling along or fighting with everything. He helped me take a giant leap in consciousness from the belief in life as an enormous struggle to the belief that life is meant to be joyous. His perspective is that you are the creator. If you're not having any fun with your creation, change it! Give yourself what you want. No one will care! If you're like me, "they" will probably be grateful that you have finally quit complaining and jumped out of your container and into the bowl. Remember the Reiki class!

I had been doing affirmations for a number of years trying to raise my self-esteem. Affirming the truth of the God within me, I am all powerful, all knowing, and one with all things. My definition of God is that God is omniscient, omnipotent, and omnipresent. In raising self-esteem, remember that it comes from *self*. We have to change the behavior that we don't like. For example, if you hate yourself for smoking, as I did, then you have to stop the behavior in order to love yourself.

Take a look at your life. What do you dislike about it? What do you have to change in order to love yourself? Do it or you will never be happy.

Whenever we have the intent to heal or create something new in our lives, whatever is standing in the way of that manifestation will arrive to be dealt with. Remember that the polarities also come into play. When you focus intently on one side of the spectrum, the opposite will come to your attention as well. Because I focused on being one with God, the memory of the "untouchable" surfaced, as it was the very thing that kept me from being all that I desired. I had to learn to forgive the untouchable and everything connected to it.

I have used that visualization technique for everything from bringing in money to creating a great relationship and losing weight. Visualization creates will power and helps you want to manifest the new behavior. Start doing the visualization, and eventually you will find your behavior changing. Remember the dream that told me it took two weeks to create something new and to be patient.

EXERCISE

Examine your life. What don't you like about yourself? Make an effort to change it. Affirm and visualize what you want to become true until it manifests. For example:

- I am loving and kind to others.
- I am courageous.
- I am creative.
- I am fabulously wealthy.
- I am healed and perfect.
- I am a non-smoker.
- I return to the center, the source of all things.
- I am calm, quiet, and at peace, and I enter the sanctuary.

Stay focused on what you want. Remember the Angel of Patience and men in red coats. Make it as real as possible. Put energy and feeling into it. Allow yourself to be worthy of all the good things in life. As you begin to focus on raising your self-esteem, remember the little flower that you are and be gentle with yourself. Do this at least once a day for at least two weeks straight.

Only on Sunday

I used to take my children all the way across town to the Unity Church in Milwaukee, where it seems to snow all the time. I'd even be willing to bet it snowed here in July—but only on Sunday. Since I was afraid to drive at that time, add snow to it, and the whole idea would put me in a state of terror.

I would do ALL of the exercises. Before I left home, I would see all of us coming home in one piece, whole and happy. On the road, I would wrap the car in a ribbon of White Light with a big bow on top. I put the White Light around each wheel constantly, while affirming, "The Lord is my Shepherd, I shall not want," all the way there and back. One day I realized that I had stopped doing all that. It was about a month later and healing had taken place. All the fear was gone. When the problem is healed, we don't even realize we're not doing it anymore—we simply stop. The new reality sets in.

Occasionally the fear will raise its ugly head again if there is more to learn. In the late seventies, I was teaching classes at the church and was feeling much better by that time, not nearly as neurotic, so I was surprised to find myself beginning to revert to my old behavior. The closer I got to the church, the more nervous I became. I inverted my thoughts and came up with the affirmation: "The closer I get to the church, the calmer and quieter I become." After using it successfully several times, the janitor walked up to me one day and asked me if I had a key to the church. I responded that I didn't. He said he didn't think that I had one, and handed me a key. Aha! How symbolic! The affirmation was the key to the church, that calm, quiet place within me where I am one with God. I found out later that the members were fighting among themselves about whether or not to institute Bingo in order to solve the church's financial problems. I felt all the negativity from the fighting in the church, which created the old anxiety all over again. Shades of Mom and Dad.

EXERCISE

To change an old habit or open your mind to greater awareness, use visualization and affirmation. Change your attitude and go with the flow. Spiritualize your life;

lift yourself out of the mundane by creating a peaceful reality. Some ideas are:

- The closer I get to_____, the calmer and quieter I become.
- The more time I spend with_____, the calmer, quieter and happier I am.
- The louder the person bangs on the piano next door, the more I can concentrate (instead of working myself into a frenzy by focusing on the noise and fighting against it).
- The slower the line at the grocery store, the more patient I become.
- The more the child next door hits the ball against the house, the happier I become.

Repeat as many times as necessary. Make up your own.

SECOND EXERCISE

Take a glass of water and hold it in your hands. Magnetize the water by blessing it. Then say, "This Holy Water makes me calm, quiet, and at peace." This Holy Water:

- brings me prosperity.
- brings me a positive, loving relationship.
- helps me to lose weight.
- heals me.
- or whatever you want.

You can use water to remember dreams by drinking a little before bed and saying, "This Holy Water helps me remember and interpret my dreams." Keep a pencil and paper next to the bed to show that you know that it will work. Drink the water twice a day. It gives the subconscious mind a nice image to concentrate on and makes it real.

chapter 5

The Greatest Problem Becomes the Greatest Gift

You Can't Heal What You Don't Feel

When my parents were divorced, I began to close in more and more to protect myself. I know now that I was a very sensitive child who couldn't handle what I felt, much less the battle raging all around me. People in the energy fields of those who are unhappy can be affected if they allow themselves to be. The emotional trauma created tremendous anxiety for me, and I began to shut down completely. Because I lived in a war zone, I built a bomb shelter. My body became the bomb shelter, and I was hiding somewhere deep inside my container, feeling very unloved and afraid to love. I grew to be afraid of everything, especially my feelings and my body. Hiding in the container was my defense mechanism. Not feeling made me feel safe, but it became the problem.

On the outside, I looked like a gregarious party girl who was having a lot of fun. Much of it *was* fun, if I could forget the fear long enough. All of this added greatly to the development of the Heebie-Jeebies. About three months after I took my first

Reiki healing class and became a healer, I saw a noticeable difference. I did some serious self-healing after that. It took about two years of healing myself and others until I realized that I felt what was going on in the body of my client in my own body. I had finally gotten strong enough inside to allow all the external shields and barriers I had created to dissolve. Slowly my defenses came down as I began to build up a trust level. Slowly I allowed myself to feel again.

Today, the way I work is through feeling in my body what the clients feel in their physical, mental, and emotional bodies. This allows me to help them to heal themselves.

SUMMARY

If you feel that you are about to panic or create a great case of the Heebie-Jeebies, there are a number of things you can do:

1. *Remind yourself that you are a divine being—all-knowing, all powerful, one with all things and all beings—and there is nothing to fear. Decide not to allow your mind to create fear of panic attacks anymore.*
2. *Breathe slowly and deeply.*
3. *Shake out, write out, or paint out the fear, grief, or anger.*
4. *Visualize yourself doing it all easily and being calm, cool, relaxed, safe, and protected.*
5. *Create a very positive affirmation, such as, "I can do this with ease and with grace," and keep repeating it until you relax completely.*

PART III

From Fear into Mastery

chapter 6

Forgiveness, the Greatest of All Miracles

There I was, sitting in my family room, wallowing in my fear and recounting the sins of my brother-in-law, Dick, blaming him for all our problems, when my friend Carol dropped in. She handed me the book *A Course in Miracles* and asked me if I had seen the book. I replied that I was sick of books because they all said the same thing. In 1977, all the spiritual books *did* say the same thing, at least from my point of view. It was a lot of "you are one with God" but no advice on how I could feel that within myself. I thought they were all nice, lovely words, but none of them told me how to be one with God. Carol invited me to be a little open-minded (one of the traits of a Teacher of God that I was soon to read about, but obviously didn't have at that moment). I took her book and opened it. The first sentence that I read was, **"If you are unwilling to forgive your brother, you do not love God."**

"Whoa!" I said. That was new information! I knew it was the truth and the information I had waited for all of my life. My life changed 180 degrees at that moment. It was never the same again. I was going to have to do something about my anger toward Dick. I was going to have to change my attitude toward him and forgive him—and probably everyone else in my life.

Here's the story about Dick: My husband, Ray, had worked in various places and then went back to work in his family business, a wholesale and retail rubber goods business, with Dick and their father. Shortly after Ray came back, Dick left the business.

Golf balls are a rubber goods product. Whenever Ray's father left town, Ray added to the golf ball line. Pretty soon they had golf balls, golf clubs, and fishing rods in the store. Semi-annually, Ray's father would scream about putting more rubber mats in the store. Ray would ignore him, as the new part of the business was making money, and added a complete line of Lake Michigan fishing equipment, which was far more interesting to him than rubber mats.

The staff had five fishing boats on the lake; one boat was owned by the company. They became the experts in the field. Ray caught the biggest Coho salmon on the lake that year, and he was in seventh heaven. He adored the business and the business was booming. Just when he was opening his second store, his brother came back into the business and sided with their father. This escalated the rubber mat fight between Ray and his father and made life more difficult for Ray. To preserve the family, Ray left the business he adored.

Instead of this helping the situation, the animosity got worse. I was so angry at my brother-in-law that I was screaming at him in my dreams, saying, "How dare you do that to your brother!" I blamed him, but Ray was angry at his parents. I had serious anger toward Dick. He and I had been close before that but now I was terrified about having enough money and our future financial security, and it was all his fault! The world as I knew it had come to an end. Nothing that could happen to him was good enough to settle the score. I was enraged. You name it, I was it. We had three teenagers at the time, and we quickly found out that our car, our boat, our money, and our friends all belonged to the business and nothing belonged to us.

Back to Carol and the book she gave me. *A Course in Miracles* talked about how we always attract what we are and never really see another's divinity or the truth about them. We only see ourselves in reflection, better known as "the illusion." The way to move from illusion to the truth is through forgiveness. I kept Carol's book for two months and devoured it. I knew that it was "The Truth," but there were parts I had difficulty swallowing. I could accept the idea of forgiveness. "I forgive you, you dirty rotten #%!!##**," which still made me superior, but see him as innocent?!!!! NEVER! See that I did that to him or that I created the situation instead of him doing that to us, that he didn't hurt us at all? That was asking TOO MUCH!! The alligators had arrived! Fear came with them in full force. I forgot everything I knew.

Nevertheless, I surrendered to what will be affectionately known from now on as the *Course*. Even with all my fear, anger, and hatred, I was willing. It seemed as though everything was taken away from us, but really, it was the beginning of receiving everything. I don't know why I didn't get the fact that one presence meant that there is nobody else but me and God, from my point of view, and that Dick and I were one and the same, and like attracts like. Fear makes separation seem logical, and guilt creates it all, but it would be a lot of years before I would understand that premise. I dove deep into my container.

Remember the bowl. I was in the depths of it, feeling quite separated from God. Fear will do that to you.

One day in my pain, I went to the Wisconsin Society for Psychical Research to heal and be healed. We did a meditation. I don't remember what the subject was, but in my meditation, I saw a baby in a womb and a butterfly in a cocoon. I saw how beautifully God took care of them until they were ready to be out in the world on their own. It made me cry, but I still wanted to fly!

I continued to read the *Course* and finally created a forgiveness exercise, as forgiveness was supposed to make the pain go away. I did it continuously with my brother-in-law.

FORGIVENESS EXERCISE

- I LOVE YOU.
- I TRUST YOU.
- I ACCEPT YOU.
- I APPROVE OF YOU.
- I FORGIVE YOU.
- I RELEASE YOU FROM ME COMPLETELY.
- BETWEEN US THERE IS NOTHING BUT GOD.
- I PLACE YOU IN GOD'S LOVING HANDS.
- I BEHOLD THE LIGHT AND THE BEAUTY OF GOD IN YOU OR THE CHRIST IN YOU, WHICHEVER IS MORE COMFORTABLE.

I once had a dream that said this exercise was the most important thing I would ever teach. It will change anything, if you do it. It does bring miracles. You are really only forgiving yourself. Remember the bowl and the Reiki class. It's what you have done or are doing to someone that you see in the other person. It's your consciousness. That's what you haven't been able to forgive within yourself. The more you hate them, the more the exercise needs to be done. A big clue is the amount of emotion you have connected to the situation.

As you say each sentence, examine your emotional reaction. In the beginning, you will feel as though it is a big lie, and it probably is. It was for me. Say it anyway. You do the exercise because you want it to be the truth, especially because it's only yourself that you are forgiving. If you continue to repeat those sentences, one day they will be true. We affirm what we want to be true, not what we feel is true at the moment. Remember the KNOW YOURSELF sign. You have to straighten it all out in your mind, then it drops down and becomes reality.

You can say, "I forgive you and you forgive me" if you want to. When you say, "I release you from me completely," know that you are only releasing the pain and the hurt of the past. The love always stays. Scan your body in your imagination. Look for ropes, chains, ribbons, umbilical cords, anything at all that is keeping you tied to that individual and/or the situation. Know that you can release it easily. Look for an instrument to cut it or a way to let it go. If you are having difficulty, ask for a spiritual guide to help you.

Often doing the Forgiveness Exercise will bring up buried emotions. It is important to find safe ways to release them so that you don't create more havoc in your life. Releasing all the negative energy around a situation makes it much easier to forgive.

Love is like gravity. It is the substance that holds all things together. It is always there—we just cover it up with our judgments, our anger, and our hatred. God is love. That's all there is. Often what we call love is really co-dependence, fantasy, or romance, which comes and goes according to our moods. Love is constant, unconditional, and the core of our being. It's what we truly are.

I found that when you send out love, trust, acceptance, and approval, it comes back to you. What goes around, comes around. When you do this exercise, you are changing your fears to love. The more I did it, the safer I felt, and the healthier I became. I began to open my heart to love and feel the love that is all around. As I worked on seeing the beauty in others, I began to see it within myself. The more wonderful and beautiful the people are around you, the more you have grown in beauty yourself.

When I first started to do forgiveness with my brother-in-law, for sure I thought he was to blame, but I was determined. Every time I heard myself recounting his sins, I would start forgiveness again. "I love you, I trust you, . . . and so on . . . " I found that I would reach plateaus and think that I was over it only to hear myself criticizing him again. I would go back to the exercise and start again. Believe me, if you are criticizing someone, you're not over it. I did forgiveness a billion times. It took me a year and a half to release the issue with my brother-in-law.

I would have periods when I thought I had actually let it go, especially if it looked as though Ray was going to get a really great job. I would thank Dick in my mind. Then if it fell through, I would be back blaming him. I went back to the exercise and continued until I really had love for him and finally accomplished the goal of changing my fears to love.

Fifteen years later, I was doing a woman's weekend. One woman there was self-abusive and could not forgive herself. I wanted to do something to help her, so we all did a regression to find out the cause of why we could not forgive ourselves. In my own meditation, I saw myself as an Attilla the Hun-type character. I was cutting off a man's head that I knew intuitively was my brother-in-law. Why, you might ask? Because he was in my way. It was the dawn of realization. I was exhibiting the same behavior in that meditation that I saw in my brother-in-law years ago. I was unable to forgive him because I was unwilling to forgive myself. Like attracts like!!! I was not the innocent bystander that I thought I was . . . the poor victim. It was all an opportunity to forgive myself, as is all of life.

Every situation allows us to let go of the past self-images we can't forgive, the ones that keep us from recognizing our divinity. They keep us tight in our containers.

One day I heard that Dick had hurt his back and was going to have a back operation. I felt badly and thought that I never wanted that to happen to him. Even though we hadn't spoken in a year, I called him and offered him a healing even though I knew that he wouldn't be interested. We spoke for an hour like old times. Forgiveness worked. A miracle happened. My fear had turned to love. Today Ray, Dick, his wife, and I all spend so much joyous time together. I can't believe I was that angry at him, but I was.

When you start to do the forgiveness exercise, you begin to release your fears and change what you attract. It's like moving your rear-view mirror. You don't see things the same way. If you're having any difficulty letting go, ask Spirit to give you a new way to look at the situation. Seeing things from a new perspective makes it easier to let it go. All forgiveness is healing. All forgiveness is letting go.

In the middle of all the brouhaha, Ray's mother had her seventy-fifth birthday. We hadn't seen the family for quite a while, as we had previously declined a few invitations. Since Ray's family wasn't great on communication, we had no idea how his mother felt about the conflict, but I was determined to end the fight. Armed with forgiveness, I vowed that we would accept the next invitation. To honor the birthday, Ray's aunt had a lady's luncheon for Ray's mother. Ray was off the hook, and once again, I had to surrender. Okay, I'll go. Our daughter was going to go with me. It would be my first foray out with his mother since the fateful day that Ray left the business. Back in those days, anything made me nervous, no matter how nice. This drove me to the edge, but I was determined to be SPIRITUAL and come from love no matter what, even if it killed me! I did the forgiveness exercise for two weeks straight. I did forgiveness with every person I thought would be there. I did it day and night, a thousand times.

When I arrived at the restaurant on the day of the luncheon, I had an interesting feeling of distance, of just being an observer rather than a participant. I had never been so calm in all my life. I felt like a plumber at a CPA convention. It was amazing! I was seated across from Ray's mother. There was a gigantic bouquet of flowers between us, so I couldn't even see her. I thought it to be quite symbolic! It took everything I had not to laugh out loud. There's nothing between us but flowers. That was divine intervention for sure. God has a divine sense of humor. I was seated with our daughter and a few young cousins and had a lovely time. Spirit really took care of me. Forgiveness changed all my fears to joy. Forgiveness creates miracles!

More Methods for Releasing Buried Emotions

Before I met up with *A Course in Miracles*, I was so angry at Dick that I picked up a belt and beat my door. Do not beat your door. You will have to repaint your door. That is experience speaking. Always hit something soft with something soft so that you do not hurt yourself or do any damage to something that you will have to clean up after. You can hit your bed but only if you don't have a water bed. Hitting is good, especially if you have pain in your shoulders or arms, but only if you're not hitting a person. NEVER hit a person!!!

Expressing anger in ways that do not hurt yourself or another person can be very therapeutic. It allows you to release the pent-up energy in safe ways so that you do not make yourself sick, create an accident, or say or do something that you might regret later. Once the energy is released, you can then tell the individual what is bothering you in a loving way rather than just screaming your head off because you can't hold it back any longer.

Screaming is a great way to blow off steam as long as you are not trying to communicate anything. People who scream when they have lost control rarely say what is bothering them. Screaming for its own sake is best done by yourself and in a private place. The car is good. People think you're singing. You don't want someone to think that you have lost your mind and cart you off to a safe place. After expressing all that elsewhere, you can quietly state the problem to the individual involved and solve it without destroying the relationship. Anger is very good if you say the right thing to the right person at the right time gently and with love.

Painting or writing out how you feel is very good. Make sure you are honest when you write what you feel. You can write a venomous letter to someone, but make sure that you burn it or tear it up so no one can see it. You don't want to create more problems than you already have.

Shaking out is my particular favorite method of releasing. Turn on some music and allow your body to shake out the pain or whatever is bothering you. Go into a place by yourself and let your body do what it needs to do. It knows where it's holding the issues. Do not judge your body!

Lying on your bed and having a tantrum just like a little kid lets go of a lot very quickly. Again, you do not want to do this in the presence of any sane adult who you are trying to impress with your dignified demeanor—they could lock you up or lock you out. It is, however, quite effective when done alone.

Another method is to lie down on your bed with your knees up and feet flat on the bed. Inhale and exhale as slowly as you can for as long as you can. This is a bio-energetic technique created by Alexander Lowen. This exercise can also bring up lots of buried treasures.

When you do exercises like these, it keeps stress to a minimum, your relationships intact, and you out of trouble or jail at the worst. There are lots of stories of people going berserk. One woman took a can of whipping cream and sprayed it all over her kitchen. And remember the eighty-four-year-old woman in a wheelchair who had a meltdown and killed her husband with her bed pan because he had taunted her for forty years about an affair he was having. I think they let her go free. For sure, a jury of all women would exonerate her. Men occasionally will pick up guns and mow everyone down.

The object of these exercises is to release all that emotion in reasonable and healthy ways so that you can make meaningful changes in your life without creating more chaos than you already have. That leads to understanding, and harmonious, loving relationships.

When you can express how you feel honestly and quietly, people listen and generally respond in kind. That adds to your self-esteem, as well.

The Forgiveness Exercise brings miracles because it lets go of patterns that you have been holding. When we're hanging out with alligators, we think the illusions are real. As an illustration, when you sit in the movie theatre, you never forget that you are sitting in the seat watching a movie. You don't go up to the screen and slash it if you don't like what they are saying. The divine part of you is the person watching the show. This is the same as the containers in the bowl. Divinity knows that it's just a drama or dream, while the ego or personality part of you is caught up in the drama.

You are holding a pattern that, unless it is broken, will cause you to continue to attract the same kind of person or situation forever until you forgive it or let it go. My "stuff" from way back when was playing in front of me at the movie "Family Business," staring me, my husband, my brother-in law, and their father. Terrible flick, I hated it! I think I had more emotion around the situation than Ray did. Dick was showing me my behavior. I was no longer cutting off people's heads, but I was quite competitive and wanted to "get ahead" back then. Isn't that cute? What a metaphor! The whole situation did freak out my ego.

I was holding that pattern and attracted it again so I could forgive it and heal myself. Anything from the past that is not released is still present and will show up sooner or later. More than anything, I wanted to heal myself so I was willing to forgive. God is an infinite creator. The drama rarely looks the same, but is the same underlying issue. Had it not been my problem, I would have actually been the innocent bystander watching the parade go by without any emotion.

Listen to the tone of your voice for more clues as to emotional involvement. Do the people in your life treat you the same way Mom, Dad, or siblings did? Are they all alcoholics? Are they all spendthrifts? Abusive? What is the pattern? Do they start out nice and then change after a while? If so, you need to do the Forgiveness Exercise—and not just once. Do it a million times or until you have really released the issue. When it is released, you attract a different type, or the person you are with will change how he or she treats you. Then you have a chance at happiness.

All forgiveness of others is in essence forgiving yourself, but sometimes it helps to actually do it for yourself. You can look in the mirror and repeat the sentences or do it in meditation by closing your eyes and looking into a pond or lake to see your reflection and repeat the following TO YOURSELF:

- I LOVE YOU.
- I TRUST YOU COMPLETELY.
- I ACCEPT YOU FULLY.
- I APPROVE OF YOU 100%.
- I FORGIVE YOU FOR ALL PAST DEEDS NOW AND FOREVER MORE.

Check out the emotional reactions you have when you say the words. Can you actually love and trust yourself? How about approval and acceptance? Can you do that? Look through your body and see if there is anything at all that is keeping the divine light within you from shining out and know that you can release it easily. Send it out into the Universe or onto the waters of life. Watch what has been a difficulty for you be transformed and go out as blessings for all humanity.

- I PLACE YOU, OR MY LIFE, INTO GOD'S LOVING HANDS.
- I BEHOLD THE LIGHT AND THE BEAUTY OF GOD IN YOU.

Remember that forgiveness brings miracles. Keep doing the exercise until you are seeing them. After doing forgiveness with my brother-in-law, I realized that there was hardly anyone I wasn't criticizing. I started doing it all the time with everyone. The more you forgive, the more you love, trust, accept and approve of yourself. Life begins to take on a new flavor. Today I am so grateful to Dick, as he brought forgiveness to me, which was the turning point in my life. I do the forgiveness exercise all the time now. It has changed my life dramatically. Paradoxically, the more you forgive others, the more the world becomes a safer place in which to live. Fears begin to disappear and confidence builds.

chapter 7

Mirror, Mirror on the Wall, Who's the Fairest?

About five years after Ray left the business, I had another incident that taught me more about forgiveness and the *Course*. I had been doing Reiki for a few years and wanted to become a teacher. Before I could become a Reiki teacher, I was asked if I was willing to give over my life to Reiki. When I very blithely said, "Yes," I really didn't know what that was going to mean or what I was going to get into. Since I thought Reiki meant the same as God, I thought I had already done that.

Surprise! On the full moon in January, after being initiated as a Reiki Master in 1983, I ran into one of my ex-fiancés whom I hadn't seen in twenty-two years and invited him over for dinner. That night he told us his story. Bill had worked in his family business until 1977, when he had difficulties with his brother. His father had already passed over.

He left the family business and sold jewelry and sporting goods for a while. At that time, he had a really good job. I was dumbstruck. I sat there with my mouth open not saying a word, which is really unusual for me, to the point where Ray noticed it. "Can you believe it?" he said to Bill. "She isn't saying anything."

What went through my head at that moment was, oh my God, *A Course in Miracles* is really The Truth, because Ray worked in his family business until 1977, had difficulties with his father and his brother, and left the business. You know the story! After he left the business, Ray sold jewelry and was back in a different sporting goods business at the time of the dinner. My thoughts were, it really would not have made too much difference which one of these characters I had married. The underlying theme was still the same, and I thought the two men were so different!

That was frightening! Believe me, if you saw these two men in a room, you would never in a million years believe that they had the same *modus operandi*. They seemed so unique on the outside. Ray, though friendly, was more of a loner than Bill, and they didn't look anything alike.

That's what I mean about God being an infinite creator. I remember hearing John Bradshaw say on television one night something akin to, "Why do I always find the depressed, alcoholic women at a party?" John had done a lot of "inner child" work. In that work, you can go back to your childhood in your imagination to see yourself in situations that brought you pain mentally, physically, or emotionally. You dialogue with the child, discover the cause of the pain, and then love and nurture the little child to heal and release what is creating the problems today.

Not only had I not done any inner work, I didn't even know that I needed to until Bill showed up. This was a shock! Like attracts like!!! I then realized that I had attracted the same exact pattern not twice, but three times. I had forgotten that my grandfather had created a family business that my father worked in. Ray worked there for a while before he left to go to work for his father. It's amazing that I could have forgotten that minor detail. So, if I had attracted that one hundred times, then this had to be my pattern! I can't tell you how scary that was.

I had to examine what I saw in them and see it *as me and my projection*. Ta da! The illusion! I always thought Ray was an entrepreneurial type and should be in business for himself. I thought I was the most independent thing around, as I had arrived in the marriage with a trust fund that was quickly dissipated through poor investments. Then I had to get really honest with myself. In reality, I was extremely dependent, first on my family, then on my husband, then on his family—not at all the independent person I thought I was.

In shock, I said to God that I was willing to break this pattern no matter what— not only for me, but for future generations (the sins of the fathers/mothers are visited upon the third and fourth generations, as it says in the Bible). I said that I was willing to support myself both financially and emotionally, neither of which had I ever done. Being willing to release the victim and support myself in myriad ways has been a constant struggle. I did the Forgiveness Exercise day and night with both Ray and Bill. It wasn't until recently, when I read a book on spiritual astrology, that I recognized that doing for myself and becoming independent was what I came here to do in this lifetime. It had always been frightening to stand up for myself. It took a long time to realize that when people were aggressive or pushed me around, they were helping me.

From that came the desire to learn to be assertive and the creation of a new affirmation: "The more I do for myself, the stronger, more powerful, and more God-like I become." I now realize that when other people *don't* help me, they are actually enabling me to achieve what I came here to do! Realizing that it is my golden opportunity to accomplish what I came here to do and that they are helping me, I have quit complaining . . . hopefully!!

This isn't necessarily true for all people, however. Maybe you have to *really* encourage others to help you, and learn to accept help. Check it out for yourself. Interestingly, once I became willing to do things for myself, other people offered to help me much more often.

Shortly thereafter, I began to teach Reiki. Classes began to spring up all over Wisconsin and in New York. I was doing quite well when Ray was laid off from his job. It was around Christmas time and I began to panic. After all, I was willing to support myself as long as he was still supporting me and the rest of the family When he was laid off, I realized that I was *really* going to have to support *myself.* So once again I was going to have to surrender on a deeper level and really be willing to support all of us. Despite our financial difficulties, Ray wanted to buy lights for the outside trees.

I was downstairs in the basement doing the dirty laundry (how symbolic!) and grumbling about his wanting to spend "my money" on Christmas lights. I was ashamed of myself, as he had always been very generous and always handed me his paycheck. Here I was acting like Scrooge! I was scared. I remembered a sentence from *A Course.* It says when you *really* want to release something, ask for a new way to look at it. I said with all my heart, "Please, God, give me a new way to look at this." I really didn't want to feel that way toward Ray. He didn't deserve it.

I have never gotten a message so fast in my life. Instantly the voice said to me, **"He supported you all those years while you healed yourself, now it's your turn to do it for him."** I said, "Okay, God, I'm willing if You make sure that we have enough." Then I really went to work. Reiki classes began to spring up like mushrooms all over the country. Ray took a few months to heal and got a new job in which he did very well. Within two years, our financial difficulties were over. Ray did a beautiful job of healing himself and today is an artist. His paintings and landscape work have brought great beauty to our home and our lives, and into the lives of all those who visit us.

The healing process continues. I am always looking to see myself in others, correcting my behavior, forgiving and releasing what I don't like, which I now know is just a mirror of myself. The forgiveness exercise and the sentences, "Please give me a new way to look at this situation, and why is this performance going on for my benefit?" are constant in my life. I'm beginning to think that there is no time that I will be "there."

The journey is the destination. And the journey is eternal . . . but it gets to be better and more fun all the time. From the experience with Bill and what he showed me about myself, I know that we are all one, and there's nobody out there but me and God from my point of view, or you and God from your point of view. If we are all one, who is the other person? Nobody!

Take a look at all your relationships, especially ex-lovers and partners. Are they alike? Is there a common theme? Remember that opposites are just different degrees of the same thing. What do you have to change to quit attracting the same thing? What drama is being played out for you?

Another illustration of the principle of illusion came to me in a very strange way. I was going to teach a Reiki class on Cape Cod, where my mother had a house. She was going to be in another part of the country at the time, and I asked her if I could stay in her house while I was there.

She called me a few times to warn me about things in the house, such as to be careful of the drapes, saying, "This and that are not in good shape; I have to work in the house, etc., etc., etc." I was getting the distinct message that she didn't want me to stay in her house. I was upset and hurt. I got so angry that I called her neighbor where my friends were going to stay and asked him if I could stay in his house instead of at my mother's. He said that I could.

I went to bed that night saying to God, "Wake me up before she leaves, so that I can call her and tell her the hell with it, I'm staying next door!"

I woke up at 5 a.m. with this message: **"You need to stay in her house and she needs to have you there."** Okay, so I won't call her. I asked my friends, "Why would I choose a mother who doesn't want me to stay in her house?" It wasn't like her at all to behave that way.

When I arrived at the house, there were all my favorite cookies and goodies waiting for me, and my mother called several times to see if I had everything that I needed. It seemed like such an about-face. I couldn't understand what was going on. The rest of the trip was lovely.

I wasn't home ten minutes when my daughter came up to me and asked if she could use my car. I was about to go into my song and dance about the terrible condition of the car and how I had to use it for my work when I realized that it was the same thing my mother had done to me. Instead of saying my usual, "No" I said "Yes," and the whole drama ended. My daughter did not ruin the car and my mother never did a performance like that again. One more time I had met the enemy and it is I. It really is a Divine Comedy! We only see ourselves in others. Sometimes it isn't so funny, though.

As I write this, ten years after the fact, when vision is much clearer, I remember the hurt I felt and the anger that came up in defense as a result of the pain.

I'm understanding today that I took that little scenario *very seriously.* I had an enormous amount of emotion connected with it. I felt very unloved. In reality, it was just the Universe showing me how I was behaving, and what I was doing to my own daughter.

Sometimes these illusions are insidious. It was very difficult for me to see the one with my daughter. God is very creative, as I said before. Today I try to be more conscious of what is happening around me. I know for sure that these dramas are my creation. A good clue is the amount of emotion connected with them. The more explosive your emotions, the deeper you're involved in the plot. Look for the message; don't kill the messenger!

We see in others that hidden, shadow side of ourselves, the part we don't want to associate with. I began to watch how people would do this. The first time I noticed it was at the office. Several of us rented office space together; most of us taught classes. One day I heard Betty, one of my officemates, say, "I always let the other teachers take my class for free, but *she* (June) doesn't," pointing to a colleague behind her back. It wasn't too long before June told me that *she* always lets the other teachers take her class for free but Betty doesn't. "Aha," I thought, "we see in the other person the same stuff."

Now I am always on the alert to what people say about each other. Beware of blaming or accusing others. Listen to what you say about them. As I said earlier, the old saying is, "You're not who you think you are, you're not who they think you are, but you are what you think they think you are." Whatever you think that someone thinks of you is what you really think of yourself. It's amazing! Only the guilty accuse! Listen to what you say about others and what they say about each other.

chapter 8

Two Men Named Dick

Some of the most important gifts in my life came from two men named Dick. Actually, they are both very nice men. The first Dick in my life is my brother-in-law who brought me *A Course in Miracles* and the Forgiveness Exercise. The second Dick in my life brought me another level of self-awareness and gave me ample opportunity to master forgiveness.

It all seemed so innocent when I saw him at a lecture about *Spirulina*, some sort of green stuff that is supposed to be healthy for you. I wasn't even that interested in *Spirulina* and was surprised when I leapt up from the dining room table and announced that I had to go to the lecture a friend was giving. I thought I was going to support my friend. I was not at all thinking that I was about to step into a massive load of Karma!—a strong love/hate relationship that gave me an opportunity to grow spiritually while fighting off my baser instincts. This is better known as moving from sexual attraction to unconditional love. I was married and he was single. I found him attractive in an odd way. From the first moment I met him, I started doing forgiveness.

I had been to see a psychic earlier who told me that if I ever lost it spiritually, it would be because of sexuality. Since my spirituality was the most important part of my life, I was not about to do that . . . no matter how much I wanted to. I did realize that fear, which was my constant companion in those days, was very much akin to sexual attraction. Both were very intense emotions that got all of my attention. There was always someone there ringing my chimes.

Much to my dismay, I completely missed the sexual revolution. First, I was a child of the fifties and no nice girl "did that." I believed the propaganda. Then I got married and couldn't run around. When I finally could put that all aside, I was too spiritual, or at least trying to be.

I loved Ray and never wanted to harm our marriage. At that time, though, I thought that everyone else was having so much fun and I was missing out. It was quite tempting. Later I realized that everyone wanted the nice marriage I had and they weren't having nearly as much fun as I thought. I was well developed as a young girl and knew how to flaunt my sexuality to get attention. They say that the angels are thrilled when we have those dazzling sexual attractions, as it's an opportunity to work out our garbage!

There is one good thing from the fifties that many women have lost today, and that was having to wait until the hot prospect called you. We girls, of course, did a lot of sneaky manipulation to try to make that happen. I'm not saying that was a good thing, but we did know that they wanted to be with us if we had to wait for them to call to ask for the date. I have a lot of clients I have had to explain this to. Often they think that the man loves them dearly because they will accept the dinner a woman offers or the movies, the trip, the car. You get the point. Often the man will then leave them for someone else he really cares about. Dick would occasionally tell me that he just wanted to be able to make a decision himself about a date.

I did the Forgiveness Exercise with him all of the time. I was determined to be able to learn unconditional love without sexuality to hide my fear or attract attention.

Dick #2 and I met at the lecture over the book table. I later found out that our moons were one degree apart and our Venuses were conjunct, for those of you who speak astrology. For those who don't, it means that it will bring up a lot of issues from childhood and the past. We had a lot of the same inner feelings and emotional reactions. We could push each other's buttons remarkably well! I played a perfect Mom for him and he played a perfect Dad for me. One sentence from him could light me up like a pinball machine and send me teetering for days.

For instance, Ray was not a big moviegoer, and I desperately wanted to see *ET*. Ray and our kids wouldn't go with me, so I asked Dick. His response was, "Dad won't take you to the movies." I was infuriated enough at him that it made me think about my behavior—that old habit of looking to someone else to give me what I wanted would creep up in odd places. I realized that I could gather my fear and go to the movies by myself. I had a wonderful time and often treat myself to a movie now. Who needs Prince Charming if you can give yourself what you want? Dick would occasionally tell me that I was defensive and behaving like a sixteen-year-old. You can imagine how well that went over. I was sixteen when my parents got a divorce. There was a lot of residue left from that to clean up. That was some of the hate part.

Another time, I had gone to a seminar out of town and met a priest who gave a wonderful class there. The priest was from Milwaukee, and I wanted to connect with him at home. I called the place where he was working to find out about the classes he was teaching. The only one I could fit into my schedule was an anger and resentment class which, of course, I thought I didn't need. The first day was about anger and the second day was about resentment. I told all my friends about it. Several of us went together.

Dick rode in the car with me. On the way over, I was saying something to him about money. No matter what I said, he didn't understand. I tried a few different ways. Then he said, "I don't care what you say. You talk more about money than anyone else I know." I could have killed him! My back started to bristle and my aura spiked like a porcupine's. *Moi*?

I'm so spiritual. Of course I don't do that. See what I mean about knowing what button to press? I made it through the class and had to teach a meditation class that night. All the while his remark was there in the back of my mind, and I was irritated beyond belief.

Our homework for the night was to write out all of our resentments. Ray was out of town that night. I got into bed about 11:00 p.m. with the plan to write out all of my resentments, even if it took all night. I knew that I had plenty of them. I started with my parents' divorce and continued till about 2:00 a.m. when I heard my self say to Dick, who was not there, "But you don't understand. My father left and he took everything with him." When I looked back at my list, almost everything tapped into that one concept that I didn't even know I was holding. I did a lot of forgiveness with my father after that.

I walked into the class the next day and asked the priest if anyone ever lived through his class. I was like a dishrag. Writing out my feelings became my second best technique for emotional release because of that experience. Start with what you know consciously and keep writing until the floodgates open. It brings up a lot of buried feelings.

My father had been my nurturer, who unfortunately left home when I was sixteen when my parents divorced. This left me with mixed emotions of deep love, defensiveness, and fear of Mom. More about her later. Then he died when I was about thirty—big time abandonment!

Even through this strong love/hate, mom/dad relationship, Dick and I had a remarkable trust level considering everything going on. It was perfect for healing. On one hand, he was a druggie and a womanizer. That was the hate part. On the other hand, he was a very compassionate and nurturing healer. That was the love part. My father, too, was a womanizer. Since Ray wasn't at all like that, Dick gave me the opportunity to release a lot of my feelings around my father and men in general. We did a lot of healing exchanges. His gentleness in the healing gave me a feeling of trust that allowed me to discuss my emotions for the first time. Prior to that I was "FINE," as you know.

For some reason, I always felt that I needed to be perfect, especially around Ray—probably that old fear of rejection stuff. Actually, Dick would force me to talk about how I felt. Learning how to do that with him saved my marriage. After I learned to express my feelings with Dick, I then started to share them with Ray.

When I read the book *Adult Children of Alcoholics* by Janet G Woititz, I realized that I had every one of the traits she mentioned. I had never considered my parents as alcoholics. No one hid a bottle behind the toilet, and no one was ever raging drunk. My parents always had a cocktail before dinner, and my father probably had the two-martini businessman's lunch.

He was a successful executive. Perfection and defensiveness were mentioned in the book. Dick would force me to tell him how I felt about him and everything else in my life. I told him in the very beginning of our relationship that there would never be anything physical between us, and I would never leave my husband. It was all very clear from the beginning, no matter how much he tried with little manipulations like, "Let me give you a massage." He was a wonderful healer and I was able to bring up a lot of buried emotion. We were both Reiki healers.

Dick was a house painter, so I asked him to paint our house and he did a beautiful job. He was clean and neat. Though not particularly punctual, he did get the job done in a fairly reasonable amount of time. A few years later, he told me that he needed money and asked if he could paint my kitchen. I agreed because he needed the money and my kitchen needed to be painted, even though I was leaving on a Reiki trip to teach in New York and leave for Greece, Egypt, and Israel from there. I had everything from the kitchen on the dining room table. I thought that Ray was going to kill me. He asked me if I was out of my mind. Probably, but I was such a good rescuer that it didn't even occur to me how preposterous this was.

When I came home and surveyed the paint job, I was horrified. Dick hadn't sanded the olive-green cabinets, and the celery color he painted on top didn't cover it and was beginning to peel. When I asked him if he would be willing to help me undo the mess he made, of course, he was unwilling to do so. That really got my attention! I thought long and hard about my need to rescue. After much deliberation, I realized that I was rescuing him because I really wanted to be rescued. Again, I thought long and hard about what I felt was lacking in my life and what I wanted.

Dick and I came together to learn a lot from each other. I sure learned a lot about rescuing and expressing my feelings. My healing work with him really helped my marriage immensely and I am grateful. I'm not sure about him, but the next time that he started whining about not having any money, I didn't offer a job as I had done before. Instead, I said to him, "I'm so glad for you. You've worked so hard to get to this place. I hope you really enjoy it!" There was dead silence on the other end of the phone. I'm sure that he hated me, the perfect Mom, for that, but he did make some big changes for himself.

The last time I saw him alive, at a lunch meeting, he asked me how I felt about him. We were always asking each other that question. Sometimes I hated the answer, but it was always healing . . . eventually. After ten years of forgiveness, I could honestly reply, "Now I really love you because there's no stuff." I looked back at him and saw golden light streaming out of his eyes. I gasped. He asked me what was wrong. I told him that I had forgotten how beautiful he was until I saw that light. Forgiveness had worked!!! As we left the restaurant, he one more time offered me a massage. I sweetly declined. As I drove away, Nat King Cole was singing "Unforgettable" on my car radio. And so he is!

I came home and left a few days later to do a Reiki class in Hawaii and then go to swim with the dolphins. Ray was with me in Hawaii for a while and then came home when I went to the dolphin workshop. We had found a postcard for Dick with a picture of a bare-breasted Hawaiian beauty on it. The caption was "Warm Hugs from Hawaii." It was perfect for him, as he was a wonderful hugger, and, of course, always interested in bare-breasted beauties We were delighted with our choice. I went on to be with the dolphins and made sure that the people running the workshop sent our postcard to him On the way home, I felt Dick's energy while I was on the plane. It was not unusual to feel his very sensual energy. I reminded him, one more time, that I wasn't going to go there and brushed him off.

When we got home from the airport, I told Ray that Dick must have gotten our postcard that day as I felt his energy on the plane. Ray told me to come into the house, that he had something to tell me. He informed me that Dick had died the weekend before. As close as we were, I did not pick up psychically that he was dying. I think that sometimes God protects us.

That evening as I meditated and wept, while I was painting out my feelings about Dick's dying and being with him, these sentences came to me: **"It was just like being with the dolphins. Sometimes they're real close. Sometimes they're real far away, but it really didn't matter because we were all still swimming in the same ocean**." There's that bowl again. It was such a beautiful sense of oneness. For a brief moment, I contemplated whether I was sorry that I never went to bed with him. I decided that I wasn't sorry at all but grateful that I was able to transmute all those sexual feelings into unconditional love. Often sex can ruin a lovely friendship by bringing up all those other ugly emotions like jealousy, fear, or distrust. I'm sure that you are familiar with them. After all my forgiveness work, I felt a great sense of oneness and peace. I realized that he came back to say goodbye when I felt his energy on the plane, and I was grateful.

I found that Dicks are really angels in disguise!! Sometimes it takes a lot of work to see their light, accept the message (and not kill the messenger), but it's worth it!

Other Relationships

If you are really being abused, get out fast. Look at the facts clearly, not what you want them to be but what is really going on. No gooey-eyed, "But he really loves me." If he's beating on you, he doesn't love you. Call the police if necessary, but GET OUT! There are safe places you can go.

If you are staying with a partner that you say you dislike, ask yourself what you are getting out of it. What's the payoff? A book titled *Women Who Love Too Much* by Robin Norwood leapt off the bookshelf onto my lap one day. It states that women often like to rescue someone because it makes them feel superior and then they don't have look at their own faults. Why are you staying? For money or security? Think about what that makes you. Think of what it does to your self-esteem.

If you think the relationship is worth saving but you temporarily hate him/her, think about what you do love about him/her. Start with that. Focus only on that and it will grow. Do forgiveness and a nice visualization about what a great relationship you have. It will change.

Part IV

Happily Ever After

chapter 9

The Joy of Relationships

A woman had invited me to the Yucatan to do a Reiki class, luring me there by telling me that people were coming from all over the world to take this class with me. Ray and I had just returned from a vacation in Jamaica. That was during the financially difficult years, but Ray was supposed to start a new job after we returned, so I said yes. After a few minutes into the trip, it was very obvious to me that no one was the least bit interested in taking a class from me. The last thing in the world that I needed at that time was another vacation! Not only was I not going to make any money, I was going to have to pay for my lodging!

The next day she took me to Coba, a nearby city. I was climbing up a pyramid in the Mayan ruins there, and about three-quarters of the way up, I psychically saw people fighting below me. I heard a voice say to me, **"So what if you were betrayed? You can always resurrect."**

Because I was there with people I barely knew, I hurriedly got up to join the group rather than keep them all waiting for me. I didn't have time to sit there all day meditating to find out who I was and who had done what to me. I assumed that I had been killed in that incarnation and they, whoever they were, did me in, but I didn't have time to get caught up in the facts.

I spent days pondering the message. I felt betrayed by her, and it made me realize that I had been betrayed many other times in this lifetime, as well. I had been abandoned and emotionally abused, and the message was right. **So what?** I'm sure that I was killed back then, and **so what?** I was still here, healthy and as happy as I would allow myself to be. I could make myself plenty miserable if I wanted to dwell on any one of those events and recreate it, keep it all alive, or I could simply say **So what?** Here I am. Still here, alive and unharmed by all the past experiences. I could rebuild my life by stopping the abuse and not abandoning myself. I could live without blame or shame—knowing that I was a beautiful, majestic, immortal, divine being, unharmed, untouched by all the negative things done to me, even death. I was as I was created to be, as the message in *A Course in Miracles* states. Nothing I have ever done, or could ever do, or anything ever done to me by anyone else could ever change that.

EXERCISE

See in your mind's eye someone who has hurt you and tell that person that you are not going to allow them to hurt you anymore. You are claiming your power and creating a new life for yourself. If we are all one, it cannot be that someone has abandoned you. Everyone and everything is here, right now. What part of yourself have you given to others? Take it back. Give yourself the love, power, or confidence, you think they took away from you. Claim it for yourself. See yourself as the person you want to be, the person you really are. Stop criticizing and abusing yourself, as well.

For the moments when you are feeling angry, frustrated, or hateful, you might like to try one of the shake-out, write-out, beat-out, or scream-out exercises.

EXERCISE

Examine your past and see how well you have been protected and provided for. Look around you and see the loving presence that is taking care of you now. If you can't see it, look again with a new attitude. Ask Spirit to show you.

Fun With Relationships

Every now and then, the drama gets too close to home and I forget all the principles. I can't see anything but alligators, and I'm not having any fun! Most of the time whenever Ray and I would go anywhere together, he would gallop ahead, stop and wait for me to catch up, and then race on ahead again. I would be walking my dutiful twenty paces behind. He has very long legs and can walk a lot faster than I can. Sometimes I would make sarcastic remarks about it. Often I felt as though we weren't ever doing anything together and I would get upset. All spirituality would fly out the window. Occasionally I was okay with it. We would often go to the theater with my brother and his wife when we were in New York. My sister-in-law walks fast as well, and my brother would sweetly walk with me. This went on for years.

Sometimes I would be really snotty about it; other times I would remind myself how lovely Ray is to me at home and tell myself to build a bridge and get over it, which is a favorite saying of my friend Judy. Attitude is everything! Once, when I decided to get really hysterical about it, I even ducked into a store in New York City to see if he would notice. This was definitely an instance where I forgot the mirror principle and the bowl, and was strictly mired in the victim consciousness of my container. Up to my eyeballs in alligators!

"You don't love me, you don't care about me, something could happen to me and you wouldn't even know. You don't love me, blah! blah! blah!" You might know that kind of scenario. I was deep in this one! Often I wanted to kill the messenger and completely forgot that it was a message.

About two years ago, we were on vacation with friends and I finally had a companion to complain to as our partners raced off without us. I analyzed the situation and decided that it was low self-esteem that made them need to be ahead of us.

After we returned from the trip, in my haste to get there before everyone else, I watched myself career through a very busy intersection on a rapidly changing yellow arrow and almost hit an oncoming car. I was deeply invested in "getting there first." Where, I wasn't sure. I instantly knew that it was quite dangerous behavior, and it was the same exact behavior that Ray had been displaying for me for years, the need to "get ahead." There it was again. I can't tell you how much I hated it!

After I realized what I was doing I stopped behaving that way and Ray never did it again. Life really is a Divine Comedy! This one took me a lot of years before I could laugh, but I finally got there. I was so invested in being a victim, feeling unloved, and blaming him. Now I try to be more careful about what I am doing. I really do want to learn this lesson once and for all. . . . No, actually it's twice.

Hopefully this is the end!

When something is happening to you or around you that you don't like, try to have the good sense to ask Spirit to tell you why the performance is going on just for your benefit. Once you recognize the problem, nobody else has to act it out for you anymore. It's as though it never happened, and it didn't except in your own mind. Ray never did anything to me; I created it and blamed it all on him.

Shadow Boxing

Even though I knew that Ray exhibited my shadow side, the following experience knocked me out. In a meditation class, I asked the group to see what was keeping them from being all that they could be. As I closed my eyes, I immediately saw Michelangelo's statue of David. I started to cry as I gazed upon it, saying, "Who could do any better than that? Why bother?" Ray's meditation showed him a scene of a volcano. He was the one chosen to be the sacrifice. That, of course, frightened him. Since Ray is an artist, I felt that I was feeling his fear and he was feeling mine. This was another one of those times that I recognized that we were playing out each other's "stuff." It was scary! We really are all one and just come to each other in different ways to heal ourselves. It proved to me one more time the importance of forgiveness and that the bowl is the Truth. Look everywhere for the unfolding drama of who you are.

Watch carefully the special people around you. What are they showing you about yourself? They are here to heal you. Accept the healing. Accept the message. Be gentle with the messenger. Remember, the principle of Aikido is that you bow to your enemy and honor them, for they are the surface upon which you polish yourself.

The Power of Healing

Occasionally something will happen that is extraordinarily enlightening. A woman who had leukemia came to me for a healing. I don't know why, but I asked her if she knew what it meant, what her body was expressing. She said that she didn't. I told her I would look it up in Louise Hay's book, *Heal Your Body*, in which she gives the mental and emotional cause for many diseases. It said that the cause of leukemia was savagely killing out inspiration. I thought that was strange, but the woman agreed. She talked about how the men in her life had told her that her writing wasn't that good, and how upset that made her. We did some emotional work around that so she could release her emotions and be healed, followed by a lot of forgiveness.

Remember that everything starts with an idea, moves into the emotional body, and then into the physical. I see in my work that many people are stuck on the emotional level. When you let go of the emotions, your body doesn't have to express them for you. Disease works the same way as those beautiful messengers in your life, letting you know how you feel and giving you an opportunity to change your mind. When you let go of the emotion, the disease disappears.

I didn't have the disease, but I did have the same feelings. I had to do some serious forgiveness myself. Talk about like attracting like! For years I held resentment toward Ray who told me, probably twenty years ago, that he didn't like my writing—not that he ever read much of it, mind you. Interestingly enough, right before the Reiki session I was about to do on that client who brought everything to light, I became very aware through a series of events that I didn't think I was as good a writer as some of the well-known women in my field.

That was quite an awakening for me. A bolt of honesty hit! I realized that I had projected all my feelings of inadequacy onto Ray, then resented him for it. He was just the messenger telling me how I felt. The revelation made me aware that I was still holding on to all that anger. For years, I channeled children's books, stories, a poem, and even a television show. Everything I sent to publishers was rejected. I finally got bored and put it all away and went on to have a successful career doing Reiki.

Years later, prompted by Spirit, I started to actually write books that I half-heartedly tried to get published. They, of course, were also rejected. This proved my deep-down belief, that my writing wasn't good enough. All of this was going on subconsciously. On the outside, I thought they were all great! Just as I thought I was so independent, only to find out otherwise when Bill, the ex-fiancé (if you're skipping around in this book—and that's fine!—see Chapter 7), arrived back in my life. No wonder the sign over the ancient Greek temples was KNOW THYSELF, since ninety percent of us is the subconscious. Learning who we are takes a good undercover detective. Learning how the personality blocks the real self and knocking the block off is a full-time job!

Then the realization came. Nothing could be published until I released my resentment of Ray and changed my own inner belief system.

I directed my client with leukemia to express how she felt toward these men and then we went through the Forgiveness Exercise. Later I did a ton of it myself. For years, I would do a few visualizations about everything being published and then quit. I knew that I had to focus on what I wanted to happen in order for the Law of Attraction to work. It is also known as various principles: the Huna principle, Makia, energy flows where attention goes, like attracts like, or what goes around comes around. Through all of my experiences with Dick, Bill, and Mom, I knew that the Law of Attraction worked powerfully on those subconscious levels, as well.

With this new awareness, I recognized that I would have to do some serious work to reprogram my computer to get my writing on the market. My desire to help people could override any inferiority feelings I held, and I knew that forgiveness brings miracles. So being willing to go for it, I started full force with affirmations, visualizations, and the Forgiveness Exercise.

In my imagination, I said to a friend, "Isn't it wonderful that all my writing has been published? So many people have been helped by the stories I have shared. I am enormously happy!" I had to do that day and night for it to sink in, even though I had given all my fears over to God for quite a while, or so I thought. When you really believe the affirmations you are saying, and that what you are trying to create is right for you, Spirit carries it out and it manifests. This book is the proof that it works!

This never ceases to amaze me!!!!! Life becomes so much nicer when you let your grievances go. Recently I took another forgiveness class titled ***Ho'oponopono***. Taught by Dr. Lew Len, it is based on an ancient Hawaiian principle that everything you see without comes from within.

That idea was the same as the ***Course***: by releasing the problem within, you can change what you see outside of yourself. I came away with a wonderful sentence from that class: **"Whatever it is in me that created this in you, please forgive me. I'm sorry. I love you."** I added, **"Please release it"** to the mix. It works wonders. It was a perfect time to keep repeating that sentence. Many times I will repeat it and also the Forgiveness Exercise. Some situations call for the whole bag of tricks.

I play out Ray's shadow side and he plays out mine. I think that our shadows are dancing and laughing at our antics. Understanding that projections create shadows certainly explained a lot to me. Every once in a while, I see a couple and wonder why they are together. When you don't know what it's all about, know that the shadows do! It's simple! They're shadow boxing.

The Great Debate

For years, Ray and I would play the same little game. We would sit and watch television or talk calmly about something, anything, it didn't make any difference, and suddenly it would become a debate. We would discuss whether we should send our children to college or should we take care of our parents if we had limited funds, or whether blue was better than green. The subject wasn't important. I would get very emotional about whatever we were talking about. Ray won every award for debate that has ever been given in high school and college. I can barely put two words together when attacked. I would end up crying and then shut down. I would become the Great Stone Face and wouldn't speak to him for a few weeks or until I forgot what we had fought about. I really didn't care two twits about the subject before the debate started.

This went on for quite a while until one day I found a book titled *Astro Analysis* by Ilya Chambertin. It talked about the astrological signs and the games each sign plays. Ray has four planets in Gemini, and Gemini loves to debate just for the mental exercise. He could argue on either side of an issue quite dispassionately, while I would jump in heart and soul. He just loved the mental challenge of it all. So I lay in wait. I waited and waited and waited until he did it again.

One night, we were seated opposite each other in the family room, talking nonchalantly. I knew a debate was about to start. Instead of getting suckered into it, I said, "Oh, no! You're not ever going to do that to me again!" I got up and walked out of the room. He never did it again, and I never heard anything about it for years. I wasn't even sure he was conscious of it. Years later, in the midst of *A Course in Miracles* class, he was talking to a woman who was whining about her husband and what he did to her, and said, "Nobody does anything to you unless you allow it." He talked about the night I told him that I wasn't going to play the great debate game with him anymore. His acknowledgment really surprised me.

A lot of people have helped me learn to stand up for myself. It took me a long time to recognize that and to appreciate and thank them instead of hating them for it. Mom was real good at ragging on me for hours on the phone, while I would just sit there in silence and offer a few *uhms* every now and then. Years later, when I finally stood up to her, it gave me a lot of self-respect, and she stopped that behavior. I'm grateful that I'm not deaf! Since I was able to shut her out so well.

Often in relationships, we play victim-tyrant roles. Sometimes it is difficult to see how the victim can also be the tyrant. The abusive tyrant criticizing or telling you how wrong you are all the time is easy to spot. Sometimes, if the victim doesn't talk about how she feels or doesn't stop the tyrant, the victim can then sit back and feel superior to the ranting of the tyrant, becoming the tyrant in her own little way. Often one person will use another to put himself down. The whining, complaining, helpless victim can hold many people prisoners. As author John Bradshaw says, "We don't have relationships, we take hostages." Let's all try not to do that anymore.

I learned a way to have better relationships when I took a dolphin training class at the Hilton Waikoloa in Hawaii. The principle of that class was to only reward the behavior in the dolphins we wanted in them. I thought that was a great idea, and I would apply it to all of my relationships. I wished that I had known that when my children were growing up. I can't tell you how much attention I gave to their bad behavior which, in their little minds, could have been construed as a reward. If you don't pay attention to it, it goes away . . . hopefully! If it's dangerous to others, to you or to them, of course you have to stop the behavior by whatever means you must use.

A number of years later, when my marriage hit a rough patch, I was contemplating having an affair and asked Spirit what to do. I heard this message: **"Honor your contracts on Earth as Christ honors God's in Heaven."** Needless to say, that took the wind out of my sails. Okay, so I wouldn't have an affair.

The Law of Attraction

One day, I decided to write out all the qualities that I wanted in a mate. I don't even know what made me want to do that. I started with all the beautiful qualities of Ray: his wonderful sense of humor, creativity, loyalty, honesty, and integrity. I added the nurturing qualities that Dick had and continued with the list.

Eventually I heard myself say, "I want an Auntie Mame-type person, the wild woman from the movie of the same name, who would take me around the world and show me the wonders of the world." That really surprised me. I didn't know that I felt that way. At that time, if I asked Ray which restaurant he would like to go to, he always picked the same one, or for a vacation, he always wanted to go back to where we had gone before. I was clearly in a rut! Knowing that like attracts like, I once again had to take a good look at myself.

I thought I was so adventurous until I realized that if a girlfriend wanted to go for lunch, I always picked the nicest restaurant close to my office. After that, I did everything possible to change. I took new routes to my office, tried new menus, and even brushed my teeth with the opposite hand. I would say to my friends, "You pick the place. I want to go somewhere new." One day, Ray picked me up at the airport from a Reiki trip and told me that he had picked out our next trip. It was the train from China to Russia. Unfortunately, the Chinese government started shooting people in Tiananmen Square and we never went, but it did prove that the energy had changed.

People will tell you that you can't change another person; you can only change yourself. You *can* change other people, but you have to change yourself first. If you have changed and it is not right for them, they will leave your life. When I first started doing Reiki, I heard this message: **"You can never hurt anyone**." I must have been afraid of healing. Years later, I was doing a *Course in Miracles* class and heard the end of the story. We were doing a meditation on power. After everyone else shared their meditation, I told them that my stomach hurt.

Knowing that the stomach was the center of fear, I figured that I had some big-time fear about power going on. Several other people also said that their stomachs hurt, so we decided to go back into meditation to find out what the fear was. I heard, **"You can never hurt anyone because everyone creates his or her own reality."** People come together to learn a lesson. It may not be in the same manner, but each learns from the situation. However, that does not give you the right to hurt some one knowingly. Remember, what goes around comes around.

The Great Marriage

Once, I decided that I wanted a great marriage. I was leaving for the weekend to do a Reiki class in Michigan, and I created a wonderful visualization telling a friend what a fabulous marriage I had. I really worked on it. By the end of the weekend, I was so hot that I could hardly wait to get home. I had visions of us making wild, passionate love. What really happened was that Ray picked me up at the airport, we went out to dinner, came home, and had the biggest fight of our lives!

He was packing his bag to leave, screaming divorce. Somehow or other we started to talk. We discussed the issues for the hundredth time but finally *heard* each other. The problems that were keeping us both from being happy together came up to be re-solved just one more time. I remember him saying, "Oh, that's what you were talking about!" I thought to myself, "Yes, only about forty-five times." I'm sure that he told me a zillion times as well what bothered him. So hang in there when that happens. It really did change the marriage. After that, we listened more carefully to one another, solved the problems, and finally did make mad, passionate love.

It could have been disastrous, but I stayed with the visualization, and it worked out for us. If Ray had not been the right person to create this great marriage with, it would have ended right there, and someone else would have eventually entered my life. Visualizations work, but you have to work them. Remember that the obstacle to having what you want will come up in your face when you start doing a visualization, but after that, it's smooth sailing, at least for a while.

The same thing happened when I recognized that deep down I really didn't want money because it gave me a good excuse not to have to go out to places that scared me. That realization came as a big shock. I thought that I really wanted to have money. I certainly talked about it all the time. I had to do a lot of reprogramming to change the fears and open to prosperity. Occasionally we have to go beneath the surface to the subconscious to find out what is blocking the manifestation. Meditation will help you discover what is lurking out of sight.

Words to Live By

Years after the creation of the "Great Marriage," life wasn't moving along as smoothly as before. I felt that Ray was hindering my spiritual growth. We were constantly quibbling over workshops that I wanted to attend and he was against. I went anyway, but it was always a hassle.

After a while I felt as though I had enough of the fight and was contemplating divorce. The big battle was in November. We seemed to argue about the workshops I wanted to attend every November. This was actually the only difficulty that we had, but at the time, I thought it was huge—after all, it was my spiritual life!

Well, it was Thanksgiving and I didn't want to divorce him at Thanksgiving, and then I couldn't do it at Christmas. We always go to Hawaii after Christmas, so for sure I didn't want to do it then.

Our anniversary is in January. I woke on the morning of our anniversary with the message that we needed to meditate together. Ray agreed, and he saw us dancing out in the stars together. I heard, **"It's not the differences between you that are important but the energy between, and when I could see the Divinity in him, it would create the Mystic Marriage in me."**

The Mystic Marriage is the union of personality with the soul—the very thing I wanted. It represented the balance of male and female that would bring me to union with God, the only goal for which I had been striving for years. That message offered me quite a challenge. Sometimes I'm more successful at it than others. It is the answer to every relationship. When we can see the divinity in others, we see it within ourselves and we recognize our union with God. So this man whom I thought was my obstacle to God was actually my ticket home. The closer I come to seeing the divinity within him, the happier I am, the better our relationship, and the more loving we both become are my new affirmations. When I can see him as divine and holy, I feel it in myself.

Try it yourself. It is the answer to the bowl. So let's offer the men in our lives a chalice instead of an apple. We can quit playing the good and evil game, and manifest what we truly are. Life will become so much more fun back in the garden.

chapter 10

The Power of Surrender

Many other things happened that also taught me the power of surrender, faith, and forgiveness. After Ray left his business, money was tight. The mortgage was due, and Ray was out of town. I didn't know how we were going to pay it. I said to God, "I don't know how you are going to do this, but I'm going to just step back and watch." Within a few days, a young man came to the door. He told me that when Ray was in the sporting goods business, he had sold Ray his stuffed something-or-other so he would have the money to go to Alaska. I think it was an opossum, Ray promised the man that he could buy it back when he returned. He asked me if I thought Ray would be willing to sell it back to him. I explained that Ray was out of town, but I was sure that he would agree to it, and told him to call later when Ray returned. When I shut the door, I started to laugh and said, "Now, God, that's really creative!!" I was really impressed! Of course, it was the exact amount of money that we needed. Magic happens when you surrender. Give over all your problems to God and watch how magic and miracles happen.

Ray and I were well on our way to a harmonious relationship, and then I found Reiki. I loved it and it helped me enormously to heal myself as I was healing others. I decided that I wanted to be able to teach it. As I said earlier, when you are initiated as a Reiki Master, then you are able to teach Reiki classes and initiate others.

My own initiation as a Reiki Master came in 1983 on Babaji's ashram in Haidakhan, India. Babaji is a guru who is worshipped by many and mentioned in Yogananda's book, *Autobiography of a Yogi*. Babaji had ascended and was able to traverse the dimensions to manifest where he chose. Even back then you didn't have to go to India to be initiated as a Reiki Master. Helen Borth, my Reiki Master, had asked me if I was willing to give up my life to Reiki when I told her that I wanted to be initiated. In my head, Reiki and God are one and the same, so I had no hesitation.

Silly me! I should have known there was a trick to it. *Reiki* means Universal Life Energy. *Rei* means soul and *ki* means energy. The original plan was to do the initiation on the Winter Solstice. We went in September.

An Italian woman by the name of Paola, who had spent a year on the ashram, came traveling through Milwaukee with Leonard Orr, the father of rebirthing. Rebirthing is a healing technique using the breath. By inhaling and exhaling through the mouth in one continuous breath, it can bring to consciousness buried emotions often associated with the individual's birth. Paola was doing past life readings and healings. In a past life reading, the psychic will focus on an individual's past and express the impressions the psychic is receiving. I had a reading with her, and she told me that I didn't love myself. It was a remarkable reading.

Then she started talking about how we were all going to go see Babaji. Immediately I thought, "Not me! You all go and have a good time. I'm not going!" I was into the *Course in Miracles* and not at all into gurus. I had completely forgotten my spontaneous past life regression that happened while I was doing yoga in my bedroom in the early seventies. I just knew that there was no way I was going to India! Or so I thought. Years later, when I remembered that regression, I realized that I had to go there in order to even begin to think of myself as a Reiki Master, to heal and forgive that old wound, and put the "untouchable" to rest forever!

Then I found out that Babaji's precept for purification was shaving your head . . . EEEK!!!! At that time of my life, I had hair down to the middle of my back, and I loved it more than God. My self-esteem was so low that my appearance meant everything to me. I could never ask anyone for a favor or anything, even from my parents, and especially not from God. What if it were wrong? Because of our financial condition at the time, I could no longer buy a new outfit to make myself feel good enough at some event. Now, my hair! Out of the question!

Well, nine of us decided to go to India in September. Helen called me up and told me she thought we should do the initiation at the ashram. I was madly visualizing my wonderful hair and how great it was that I didn't have to shave it! I was coming home with my hair—or so I thought.

The fourth day at the ashram was D-Day. You either asked permission to keep your hair, shaved your head, or left the ashram if Babaji said that you had to shave your head. It was also the full moon. The full moon is the most spiritual time of the month, as the energy is the strongest. Groups meet all over the world at the time of the full moon to meditate in order to bring into themselves the energy to transmute their own beings and send it out as light and love and peace for the planet. I had been doing full moon meditations for about a year and thought I would, just might, mind you, shave my head on the full moon, if I had to. I didn't know that it was D-Day. The night before the full moon, I went to bed asking Spirit what to do about my hair. I woke up in the middle of the night with this message, **"If you would do this, you would know forever that you had given everything over to God."**

I lay there and cried for quite a while. I asked for a second opinion or someone else to talk to. When none was forthcoming, I got up reluctantly and went to the barber. He started in the middle of my head with a straight razor, and in minutes I was bald. I threw my hair into the Ganges and never looked back. I determined right there that I was only going to do what was right for me from then on. The next day I was initiated as a Reiki Master, in all of my startling glory, at the ashram by Helen.

After I had my head shaved, I started saying, "Okay, God, now this is what I want. I want to be at one with You. I want to be at one with nature." I finally had enough self-esteem to ask! I had been stripped of my money and my hair, but in return, I got self-esteem and was beginning to love myself. There's nothing like surrender, as horrible as it seems at first. It works!

To love yourself, give your life over to God. When you give everything to God, it is reciprocated. Your life will change dramatically!

Babaji

After my Indian adventure, I saw myself standing in the fire and Babaji was holding me in his arms. I received the following message: "If I would know at all times that God is holding me and protecting me, I would see the ups and downs of life as a great adventure," somewhat akin to a roller coaster.

People pay good money to go way up in the air and down to the pits again on roller coasters, to be scared to death, something like instant success and failure. I realized that I, for one, prefer to go from high to higher. I didn't enjoy the pits— particularly the periods with no money at all, which was what I was going through at that time. I was only waiting for it to be over, for our money to be restored and everything to be normal again. I wasn't having fun and didn't see it as a wonderful adventure at all. In retrospect, I learned a lot about how protected I was during those times.

EXERCISE

Affirm: **"Today I will watch how God protects and provides for me in all that I do and in all that is done for me, and truly see God at work in my life."**

Look back in your life and see how you have been guided and protected. Or, if you are like me, pushed and prodded to grow. Sometimes I go kicking and screaming all the way, but it does get easier as time goes on. Look at all of your blessings and be grateful.

Prosperity Reigns

Money and security issues were enough to give me the Heebie-Jeebies. Reiki was always trying to teach me to trust. When I really needed money, I would have classes of thirty people in New York. Sometimes classes could evaporate into thin air, yet one class grew from eight people to twenty-two overnight. If Spirit gave me a rest period, I always had an undercurrent of doubt. I was worried that the world had forgotten me, but sure enough, people would start to call again. Spirit never deserted me.

I had been teaching in Japan twice a year for about eight years when I received, *The Abundance Book* by John Randolph Price, at one of the Ramtha events. It is a forty-day prosperity program. The theme is that your prosperity comes from

God; you need to keep affirming that in writing for forty days. I worked at it very diligently. I was starting to get nervous about Reiki being able to support me as more and more Reiki Masters appeared on the scene. My mother had offered me money prior to that but had some sort of excuse and withdrew her offer, which made me angry enough to think, "To hell with her. I will become my own mother and make my own money!" I was particularly annoyed since I had never asked her for anything, but I would have loved the help.

I had always made a great deal of money teaching Reiki in Japan, but around the first of the year, my contact, Cathy Clark, said that she wasn't sure I should come because there were now a lot of Reiki Masters. I told her that I had to come as I was going to initiate a woman as a Reiki Master. Because of that, it would be all right financially and not to worry.

In May, on the thirty-sixth day of Price's prosperity program, I left for Japan. When I arrived the next day, I found out the woman had decided that she didn't want to become a Reiki Master. There went my security! Tokyo was the most expensive city in the world, and I paid all of my own expenses, but I still had a few people who wanted Reiki III. Reiki I is a class in which the student learns how to do laying on of hands energy healing. In Reiki II, the students learn the techniques of distant and mental healing. In Reiki III, the students are prepared for mastery. In each class, the students receive initiations that open them to receive the energy. Each class is more powerful and, of course, more costly. Teaching Reiki III in Japan would at least pay all of my expenses. On Day 38, only one person came for Reiki III. At that point, I wanted to cry and go into fear, but I kept affirming that my prosperity came from God. It didn't come from Reiki classes or Mom. I mumbled, "I trust you, God," a few thousand times under my breath all the way to the Reiki demonstration I was giving that night. Usually there were about thirty people in the audience, but that time there were only ten, and most of them had already taken my class. They had come to visit me. That was lovely, but I needed students!

They did tell us at the center that a Japanese man had come there that afternoon to take the Reiki III class. He had taken I and II from a Japanese teacher and didn't know to call Cathy, as that class was being held elsewhere. One of my Japanese students thought she could find his number in the phone book.

I fought back tears all the way home that night but kept reminding myself that I had wanted to take a deeper step into Spirit and this was the way to do it. "I trust you, God. I trust you, God." was my constant mantra. There were ten people signed up for the Reiki I class. It wasn't the fifteen or twenty-five that I was used to, but it was okay.

On Day 39, only six people came for the class. It took all that I had not to cry or panic. I wasn't sure which would come first. It actually was a lovely class, nicely balanced with three men and three women, three Japanese-speaking and three English-speaking people. I held myself together and picked the Angel Card of JOY. I said to the angel, "There has to be Joy here some place. I just have to find it." It was a wonderful class with very interesting people. I kept focused on JOY all day and all night.

That evening, Cathy called me to say that she found the Japanese man and he was going to come to class the next day. Somehow I made it through the night. I kept affirming that I had asked for this challenge and I would trust God no matter what happened. I kept reminding myself that my prosperity came from God. I had never worked so hard to keep my focus in all my life!

Sunday, Mother's Day and Day 40, when I got to class the next morning, the entire room was filled with my students who had already taken Reiki I. They were there to see me and to hang out in the energy. I thought to myself, "Look what JOY can do." Cathy announced that there would be another Reiki III class on Monday as it was a national holiday. The Japanese man still wanted to take it. Another woman said, "Oh, Monday, I can do it that day but only in the afternoon." Cathy also announced the Reiki II class the following weekend and the availability of healing times. Many people signed up for healings and twelve people signed up for Reiki II, so I went home with my usual amount of money. That night I called my mother and wished her a happy Mother's Day with love in my heart.

The best part was that I spent the morning alone with the Japanese man. He felt as though he really hadn't received Reiki II, so I went through the Reiki symbols with him and he told me the origin of the symbols I gave him. He also told me where Dr. Usui, the man who rediscovered Reiki, was buried and how to get to the holy mountain where Dr. Usui received Reiki. That trip was equally as wonderful as all the rest of them had been, and it was not my final trip there.

I wasn't home very long when a student from New York called to ask if I was coming back to New York to do a Reiki class. She said that she had been in my classes and wanted to become a Reiki Master. I told her that I had no plans to come there at the moment and that my contact who had set up the classes before had died. She said she would be delighted to set up classes for me and that she had a radio program and would be happy to promote classes on the program. We arranged a few trips to New York for me to do classes and a time to initiate her.

At the end of the conversation, she said, "By the way, I decided to drop my stepfather's name and I now call myself Mother Khoshhali."

I asked her what she would like me to call her.

She said, "Oh, you can call me Mother."

It took everything I had not to laugh hysterically! I remembered my proclamation almost a year earlier about becoming my own mother and giving myself plenty of money. Well, I created a new one. "Mother" Khoshhali brought me to New York every two months for about a year. I never could call her Mother, but I told her the story later and we had a good laugh about it.

At the time, my own mother was in the first stages of Alzheimer's and needed help. She began to think that she had no money for food and therefore wasn't eating. She was independent, feisty, and paranoid. I saw in her the same behavior that she had always exhibited, but it was now to the third power. I recognized that it really never had anything to do with me, it was just her fear, but I hadn't known that as a little girl. It was obvious that my brother and I had to help her. We tried everything to get her to sign a power of attorney for us. One moment it seemed as though she was going to sign it and the next moment she would attack us.

Finally I said to God, "I surrender! I can't take this emotion anymore. You take care of her. I quit." I felt like a ping-pong ball jumping back and forth between the polarities—elation if I thought she was going to sign and fear if it looked like she wasn't. I decided to forget about it. I did a healing on her, took her to an art gallery and out to dinner, and then took her home. After that, I came back home from New York, where my mother lived. It turned out to be one of the nicest visits that I had with her during those years.

Right before I was about to return to Japan, my uncle called me and told me that my mother wasn't cashing the checks from the trust her father had set up for her and her siblings for their lifetime. He wanted to give it to us! My uncle initiated all the papers that needed to be signed. Along with them was the power of attorney we needed. On my next trip to New York, my brother and I took Mom to her attorney and she signed all the papers easily. Surrender works! It was a wonderful miracle.

I finally got the carrot she had offered a number of times before, but always managed to find a reason why she wasn't going to give us any of the money that was ultimately to come to us. She had dangled it in front of this donkey for so many years. Prosperity at last! We could now take care of her without fear of not having enough for ourselves, as well. The exercise had worked!

Prosperity is a funny thing. My father had the prosperity consciousness in our family but my mother had the money. She had inherited hers, but my father made and spent a lot of money. My father lived like a king and my mother, through the years, became more and more frightened about money until she didn't think she had any. We would give her plenty of cash, but even a thousand dollars in her purse couldn't convince her that she had enough money. Alzheimer's is a long, painful disease, but it allowed me to care for her and forgive her; it gave me an opportunity to heal and change all my fears of her to love. Once you have been initiated into Reiki, the good thing is that it never lets you stay in a rut. The bad thing is that it never lets you stay in a rut, so the adventure of growing with Spirit and becoming all that I can be continues. Conquering my fears and mastering my life is always a challenge. Life gets to be much more fun. The other side of the illusion is JOY!

If you are dealing with the lack of money in your life, do visualizations and affirmations about how fabulously wealthy you are and remember that you give it to yourself. Open yourself to it. If there's guilt, find out why and get rid of it. Love yourself enough to give yourself all that you want. Go into meditation and ask Spirit. Be charitable, as what goes around, comes around, and above all, trust! Try Mr. Price's forty-day program. It works!

chapter 11

The Divine Comedy

The following are sayings, revelations, and stories that have inspired me and helped me learn to love myself.

The Circle of Women

Once in a spiritual development class, I led the group in meditation to go to the Circle of Women to see what they could discover there. I didn't know what that meant. When contemplating what meditation to do, I heard Spirit say, **"The Circle of Women."** I was surprised at what I received. I saw in my mind's eye a group of women sitting around a fire, then I rose up from the fire into another dimension. I seemed to go straight up above them and saw a lot of sand and what seemed like a group of women living alone on an island. Suddenly I saw a canoe paddle. A large man picked up the paddle and pushed it into the sand, claiming all of the land for himself and, naturally, all of the inhabitants. He made slaves of all the women and dragged them away in a net made of ropes.

After a while, the women tired of being slaves. They surrounded the man and trapped him with his own net and freed themselves. Still in the meditation, I returned to the circle of women around the fire, told them what I had seen, and said to them, **"Women need to be their own authority."** I then ended the meditation and brought the class back to the present and shared the experience with them. I had never experienced a meditation within a meditation before. It was very exciting to me.

Women especially, but men as well, need to be their own authority. Look at the men around you, how they treat you, and your reactions to them.

Meditate on what you are doing that you don't like. What are you doing in order to please someone else? Give yourself permission to be yourself! Empower yourself. Do what you want to do. Be what you want to be. Visualize yourself being all that you can be and doing what you want. You have a right not to be manipulated, to set boundaries for your life. Once you become your own authority and empower yourself, not only do you free yourself, but you also free your partner and those around you. Imagine how much easier life will be for others when they know what you want and that they don't *have* to take care of you. They will enjoy being with you that much more when it is an equal partnership.

I remember a time a long time ago when Ray and I were loudly discussing something, and he asked me what I wanted. I screamed, "Freedom!" I was pretty shocked at my intensity and my answer. That was long before women's lib. Years later, a friend of mine came into town and called to see if I could meet him for a drink. I said, "Sure," and left to go meet him. On the way there, I recalled my screaming incident and realized that I had always had freedom—I just never gave it to myself. I was always too afraid to be free. I worried about what somebody else would think, was it right, if I was good enough, or whatever stupid thing I dreamed up to sabotage myself. I was good at that.

As I've said before in this book, the conscious mind is the masculine part of us. That is the decision-making part. The best example would be a computer programmer who decides how to program the computer to get the best results. The feminine part of us is the hard drive, or the inner workings of the computer, which takes all the programming it has been given, mixes it all together, and comes up with a conclusion. Often men and women take on those roles and show you what you do to yourself. Men can show you how you think, or how you are programming or not programming yourself if the roles are not working at all, and women can show you your emotions and how you are feeling. It's all so much fun! It definitely gets so much more enjoyable when you are ahead of the game and know what's going on. The following are a few experiences that taught me how to make it all more fun.

Sun Bear

Three shamanic weekends were being held at the same time in the area. A shaman is a medicine man, part of the Native American tradition. I decided to choose the one that Sun Bear was offering because he was doing a sweat lodge and I wanted to do that. I wasn't sure what it was, but someone had told me that I needed to do it and that it was very purifying. It's done in a tent where they light a fire and then pour water on the coals to create steam. You do a lot of releasing of buried emotions with it, following a Native American tradition. It's much like a steam room with ritual. It's a sacred part of their tradition.

I had a psychic reading before I went. The woman told me that she saw me sitting in a circle of women and crying. I was all excited because I thought I was going to get in touch with my Native American inner feelings and remember being an Indian. Well, here's what really happened. It never is what I think it will be.

I went with my friend Sherry. We set up a tent for the night—a hot, sticky, buggy night. I woke up to discover that I had my period. As we walked to the ladies' bathroom, someone said, "Sun Bear won't let you in the sweat lodge if you have your period." I was disappointed but decided to keep quiet about it and just see if that was true. We were told to go sign up for the sweat lodge. Sun Bear walked by me and nodded to me. I figured that was my go-ahead sign. I really wanted to go! That's why I chose his weekend.

As we were standing outside waiting to enter, Sun Bear gave a speech about women being in their power when they had their period and that's why they couldn't go in. I fervently prayed to God saying, "If this is right for me and I'm not going to harm anyone else or myself, please give me a sign." A gigantic butterfly came and hung around right in front of my face. I knew that was my answer. I went in and sat right behind Sun Bear.

Nothing happened. It was pleasant but not earth-shattering. I didn't hurt myself or anyone else.

The next morning, I was sitting in a circle of women. A beautiful woman named Amy talked about the Native American tradition of celebrating the young girl's entry into womanhood. The young woman enters the Moon Lodge to spend a few days. All the other women in the Moon Lodge love, nurture, and pamper her while she is menstruating. I sat in the circle and cried.

I got my first period when I was at camp. I was eleven. I didn't even know what it was. I'm sure my mother must have given me a book about it, but the stain in my pants didn't look like blood. It disappeared after a few days, not to resurface for a year. Here, in the circle, it was the gentleness and caring of each other that made me cry. Nurturing and gentleness by women was quite alien to my childhood experience.

Amy then asked the group to talk about how they were treated at work when they had their period and any experiences around it that they wanted to share. Some of the women were really angry because of the derogatory remarks they had received from their male bosses about "women's issues" when they asked to get excused from work. A few women said the men would roll their eyes, giving them the impression that they had made it all up to get out of work. Many felt that the men were afraid of the power that women held to be able to give birth, and for sure most of them didn't understand it and that could scare them.

Then came the big question: How did you feel when Sun Bear told you that you couldn't go into the Sweat Lodge. I very quietly said, "I went anyway. I'm not a rabble-rouser and I certainly didn't do it to be disrespectful. I did it because it felt right for me to do."

A number of women came up to me afterwards and congratulated me for doing what was right for me. I still to this day don't understand Sun Bear's reasoning. Maybe it is just men's fear of the feminine and the power of birth that we hold, and a way to dominate women.

Following the women's group, we had a medicine circle. As we were all sitting around in the circle, I kept batting at a bug that I felt hanging around me. My friend Sherry leaned over and told me that a butterfly was hovering. I looked up to see a butterfly land on the back of my right hand. I was thrilled! I very slowly and quietly turned my hand over. I thought it would really be cool to have it sitting in the palm of my hand. It got as far as the side of my hand and flew away.

Since butterflies are the symbol of transformation, I knew that something major had happened to me that weekend. On the way home, I remembered that whenever things weren't going well with me, an Indian chief would appear in my meditations. He would be standing there with his arms crossed with a very disapproving look on his face. He never came back into my meditations after that, so in some way, I became my own authority. It all made sense that I had to do it with an Indian chief. Looking to the guidance from within as your highest authority is always the safest way to live.

Moving from the concept of God being without—a man standing on a cloud making black marks against my name—to God being the power that created all things, all knowing, all powerful, and everywhere present within as well as without, sometimes still eludes me. I think I know it intellectually, but occasionally I go into fear and forget that I am the God judging me. If you find yourself in that predicament, observe your behavior and change the behavior you think is being judged. You will then begin to love yourself. Be your own authority.

The Call of the Dolphins

From the moment I heard from a friend that you could swim with dolphins, I was hot to go. I went first to Dolphins Plus, a place in Florida where they have dolphins that are penned in so that you can swim with them. There is a hiding place within the pens where the dolphins can go to escape humans if they want to. I had a magnificent experience because there was a great deal of interaction with them. They made me into a dolphin sandwich, with one swimming above me and one below.

When I asked them to teach me how to play, a dolphin came right up to my mask and opened his mouth, showing me all of his teeth, pretending that I was lunch.

He swam away after that. It was very funny. I laughed out loud, and then got water in my mouth and got very flustered, which made it even funnier. One dolphin even tried to make love to me. He wrapped his penis around my knee, and rocked me like a chicken on a spit. The trainers watched to make sure that I was all right. It was wonderful. I loved it!

The next time I went there, the dolphins ignored me completely, choosing a younger companion! Just like a man! It might also have had to do with the fact that I had decided that I wanted to touch them. After all, I was a "Reiki Master." My energy was good. I wouldn't hurt them. We were told that you must keep your hands behind your back, away from them. The way to give to the dolphins was to not want anything from them but to allow them to come to you—a difficult task for me. "Letting" was not my best act. Sure enough, this time when I wanted to touch them, it was the curse—the kiss of death.

After swimming with the dolphins in captivity, I decided I didn't want to do that to them anymore. I only wanted to swim with them in the ocean, where they were free. I signed up to go to a workshop with Joan Ocean, a lovely mermaid who takes people out into the ocean to swim with the dolphins in Hawaii and other parts of the world.

Six other women came to the dolphin workshop, as well. One evening, early in the week, we did a New Moon Ceremony. We were supposed to do an exercise to eliminate something in our lives. Immediately I heard the voice say, **"I release the hatred toward my mother."** So I wrote that on a piece of paper and we burned it. I told the group that it was anger I was releasing because I was ashamed of having hatred, but as I got to know them better, I told the truth. I did a lot of forgiveness with my mother that week.

The dolphins were either absent, far away, or very deep during that period. We were all anxious for them to come to be with us and would search for them daily. I felt that the ocean was the same as the Divine Mother. Finally, toward the end of the week, I said to Her, "I'm willing to open up to receive you and all of your gifts." I figured out that what the dolphins gave me was the feeling of joy and excitement that I hadn't experienced since I was a little child at Christmas. I realized that I was going to have to give that joy to myself, so I decided to forget the dolphins and go snorkeling. The fish were glorious. I swam into a pod of little bitty silver fish. They were all around me. It was a heavenly experience. It was as joyous as being with the dolphins.

We decided to become our own dolphin pod. We swam together, enjoyed the snorkeling, explored the coast, and loved and cared for each other. We found the joy of the dolphins and the ocean in being together. I went home feeling exuberant and transformed, even though I didn't have the experience of my dreams with the dolphins. We all got the message, and have continued to be loving friends.

Filled with all that love, I came home to find out that my dear friend Dick had died. It marked a big transition in my life. Prior to that, I always searched for friends in men, as Daddy was safe and had been my nurturer. I'd had women friends before, but this experience allowed me to open and trust them fully. It was my first experience of finding the Joy of the bowl.

The following year, several of us returned to Hawaii, and the dolphins were there to greet us. They stayed and played all the first day, and they interacted with us the entire week. I had never seen so many dolphins. It was wonderful. As they flipped and jumped out of the water, it was the greatest show on Earth!

The dolphins taught me to release the anger and hatred toward my mother, as well as to be open to all women and to receive all the treasures of the world. I learned to make the Universe a wonderful and joyous place in which to play. I found that when I could love my mother, I could open to prosperity. The feminine principle brings forth the substance of God.

Three years later, I went to swim with the dolphins in the Red Sea. A dolphin came up and put his mouth around my left hand and swam all the way down the left side of my body. As he did that, I could touch his whole body. Finally my dream came true.

Make a special effort to open yourself to receive the gifts of the Universe. You can't receive if you're not open to them. You will never find them within the container. If you don't feel the gifts or see them, ask for them. Keep looking for beautiful things in your life.

You Are the Master of Your Destiny

A young man came to interview me about Reiki for his university's newspaper. He asked me all the appropriate questions about healing. At the end of the interview, he said, "I just have one last question. Imagine that an extraterrestrial is standing in front of you. What would you say to him/her/it about Earth? Would you recommend that they come here to visit or to live?"

I closed my eyes and pondered his question for a moment. I started to cry when I saw beautiful, majestic mountains, then beaches and the ocean. "Oh, yes, come here," was my response. "It's so beautiful." I cried at the beauty of it and then I thought of people, and the energy dropped a few thousand degrees. I then heard myself say, "It's a great place for a master to know who he is."

We learn who we are by the world we have created around us. Remember that effectiveness is the measure of truth from the Huna principles we discussed in Chapter 3. The effect is what you have manifested. Who are you?

What have you manifested here? Is your world a place of peace and joy? Are you having fun here? Have you created beauty in your life? If you haven't, you can change it! What isn't beautiful? Master, your world is your canvas. Create a beautiful picture!

Maybe It's All Just a Dream

I was doing a class on past life regressions. The plan was to go back to a time when you knew who you *really* were. In the regression, I directed the class to go down in an elevator to that time. When they walked out of the elevator, they would see a scene in front of them.

When I walked out, I saw a jungle scene in front of me, with a plastic wall between me and the scene. Aha! The separation, I thought. I walked forward through the wall into the forest. I continued to walk and suddenly someone was in front of me with a movie camera filming me as I was walking forward.

Another Aha! The projection, I thought. We only see what we project out onto the Universe. I kept walking right through the person filming me. I saw a scene in front of me of a couple with a baby. That was the third Aha! I realized it was the beginning of creation, the union of male and female bringing forth the child.

Suddenly it all went dark in front of me. I heard a voice say to me, **"I am a thought in the mind of God."** I thought that was awesome! We are all within our creator. All that God is, we are. Once again the Bowl of Truth was in front of me and my dream. Walk through the illusion of your life. Who are you really? Remember who you really are, created in the image and likeness of God.

Death—The Greatest Illusion of Them All

Our grandson was very ill and about to undergo an operation for cancer. Before we left for Hawaii, where he and his family were living, I saw the following in meditation. A shaman, a medicine man, was shaking a rattle for all he was worth, and a dead crow was lying on the ground. As he shook the rattle, the crow began to vibrate and to lift up off the ground. The crow would lift up and fall back down. The shaman shook the rattle harder, if that was possible. I felt as though my whole body became that rattle. Suddenly another crow came in, and they both flew off together. I heard Spirit say **"Remember, it isn't real."**

I knew this was telling me that my grandson's illness was not real, and death wasn't real, it was only an illusion. If there is nothing but the life force, how can death be real? That message helped me all week while we were there with our family. I prayed, sent healing, and held the energy of that thought—it isn't real!

The operation took half the time allotted for it, and two days later he was down in the playroom. While we were in Hawaii, I was contemplating the message that "it isn't real" and realized that the radiation and the chemotherapy that they were planning wasn't real either. This allowed me to accept my children's belief system and honor their choice, no matter what I believed, because I was a firm believer in natural healing and they were into drugs. I witnessed extremely loving doctors and nurses who truly cared for my grandson's well-being and that of the entire family. That one message enabled me to change my entire attitude toward the medical profession, which before was, "They don't know what they are doing."

Seeing a situation from a new point of view really helps you to let it go. I didn't realize until I went through that experience how much fear I had about illness and doctors. I should have known that, since *A Course in Miracles* says that you only teach what you need to learn. I feel that the worst of it is over and that our grandson is well on his way to perfect health. Today he is nineteen years old and going to college.

Remembering that people are all right no matter what happens to them is not always easy, but it's all very simple. Whatever you are faced with, it helps to remember that it isn't real, only an illusion. The divine part of you lives forever.

I know that when you are surrounded by alligators, they seem quite real. That's the time to remember who you really are and the bowl. There is nothing real but love and life. When you see a dandelion growing up in a crack in the cement—between a rock and a hard place—you can see how strong the life force is. It is within you. It can overcome anything. Trust it!

The Great Symphony

In the Full Moon Meditations I do, the information I use comes from the book *The Symphony of the Zodiac* by Torkom Saraydarian. He states that as long as we are enslaved on a personality level, we are never free. Those attached on a physical level will be stuck in their habits and addictions and enslaved by those who are also enslaved on a physical level. Emotional attachment leads to hang-ups, and those people who are attached to people or things on an emotional level will be enslaved by others who are also attached on an emotional level. Mental attachment leads to fanaticism. People who have mental pride or attachments will be enslaved by other fanatics. The battle of the wits ensnares everyone. Some wars are fought for these reasons.

Check your feelings about religions and religious ideas, races, and nationalities. Find the hidden beliefs that are lurking there, keeping you from being at peace. If you're just a thought in the mind of God, what thought do you want to be? Love?

Unity? Peace? Certainly not war, anger, or frustration. Those thoughts just keep you separated from God and dancing in the illusion. Forgiveness gets you back to the truth.

I did an exercise once in which I met with inter-dimensional beings. The group I saw looked like bubbles. They were all happy and joyously met with me and other bubbles like themselves, blending and playing with us. They interacted so harmoniously with me—it was a wonderful feeling. I realized that all the intellectual analysis and judgments that I usually have were missing. It was just pure enjoyment. I felt so free, lighthearted and easy. I loved it.

There are a billion reasons for us to hate each other, to be angry and fight about everything, from what others look like to what they have, what they think, what they believe, or what they did to us. There is only one reason for us to look beyond all of the comparisons and separation and to love each other. The only reason to do this is because it is the only thing that brings us love. It is the only way to happiness and peace.

I Am That I AM

I was at a spiritualist conference where a priest by the name of Dean Merrick offered a Death Meditation. It intrigued me, so I signed up for it. About thirty of us were lying on the floor as he directed us to see ourselves at our funeral. He suggested that we begin to let go of our possessions, our bodies, our careers, our successes and failures, our relationships, one by one, our self-image, and our fears. I realized that I had a very difficult time releasing my fears, for they made me what I was. It seemed odd, but I remembered the *Course in Miracles* stating that the ego represents that part of us that is frightened and feels separated from God. I finally let my fears go along with my body. It was the first time I had ever been able to see myself without a body of some sort.

All I could see was gray. It seemed that there were other consciousnesses in the gray mass that I was a part of, but nothing and no one was distinct. I then began to ask, "What am I?" and the answer was **"I am that."** Then I had the thought that **"I Am That I Am,"** God's answer to Moses when Moses asked God who was speaking. Slowly Dean called us to return to our bodies. I decided that I wanted a new body with less fear, and certainly better looking. I resolved to return with more love and different attitudes.

As we slowly brought our awareness back to the room, Dean began to show slides of people from all walks of life. He passed out wine and we all shared a loaf of bread as most of us sobbed and hugged each other. For me, it was truly a Holy Communion and one that I will never forget. I felt as though I had touched the Divine. We are truly only a thought in the mind of God. There is no separation; we are all one. Keeping that reverence is something I wish for forever, even when a child spills the spaghetti sauce on my white rug or a beloved friend points out my faults.

I Am

Just recently I experienced in a different meditation the sequel to the I Am That I Am revelation that I had so long ago. I was leading a meditation in *A Course in Miracles* class and asked the group to see themselves in the Temple of Enlightenment to discover what would lead them to enlightenment. In my own meditation, I saw in my mind's eye a person climb upon a throne holding a scepter, saying, "I am the ruler here." Then I started hearing the words **I AM** coming from all over.

They were above my head, below me, from in front, and on every side. It seemed as though the sound came from everywhere. The same powerful force was manifest in my body. I remembered the experience from long ago when, as a teenager, I was literally in the closet, as I described in Chapter 3, but this time I knew the I AM presence was within me—the life force that is all knowing, all powerful, and everywhere present. This force or energy, the I AM presence, is what I call God or nature. It is the treasure within. It took a long time to get to that understanding. Hearing the words I AM everywhere made me realize that there is nothing but that. It filled me as well as all people and all things, and I should be very careful of what I included with those two words, as I could create anything with this energy. It definitely showed me the bowl one more time. If we are one with God, then truly we are everyone and everywhere.

Aloha: To Love Is to Be Happy With

I went on a meditation retreat to Hawaii. The first day of the retreat we went to the Place of Refuge, sacred grounds of the Hawaiians. If a convicted person could reach that place, he or she would be free. We wanted to tap into the energy of the Kahunas, the ancient healers and Hawaiian Masters. I asked them to teach me of their wisdom. They told me that to work with them, I had to show everyone that they were forgiven. In meditation at a different time, the voice said to me, **"To love another is to show them the Beauty of their own Divine Soul."** Beyond their behavior, beyond the appearance of form, beyond their self-image lies the truth, the God within—that beautiful, radiant star. Work on the forgiveness exercise. Keep doing it a billion times until you have forgiven everyone. It's a full-time job. It's the only path to love, peace, and happiness.

U.S. Airways

One day I was traveling from New York to Boston with a group of friends. As we approached the gate where the plane was supposed to leave, there was a buffet table set up with a tray of fruit, cheese, and crackers, and a bin of soft drinks. There was no sign on it saying who it was for or why it was there. I got up and walked around it for a few minutes.

After a while, a man went up to the table and helped himself. Seeing this, I went up to him and asked about it. He told me that he didn't know what it was there for, but he was helping himself and why didn't I? I made up a nice plate for myself and went back to my friends, explaining that none of us knew what it was for but he and I had helped ourselves and why didn't they. Soon other people began to help themselves and everyone was having a good time.

When we got on the plane, we asked them about the buffet table. The flight attendant told us that U.S. Airways was inaugurating their new shuttle service between New York and Boston and they hoped we liked it. This made a big impression on me. The phrase from the 23rd Psalm kept running through my head: "He prepareth a table before me in the presence of mine enemies." Now I wasn't with enemies, but I kept thinking that God gives it all to us and all we have to do is walk up to the table and help ourselves. Be open to receiving the goodness and love of God that is ever present, and that's what Jesus was trying to tell us. I am the only one responsible. My judgments and lack of self-worth keep me from having what I want, from eating from the banquet table that life is offering.

All I have to do is open myself enough to learn to receive and allow miracles to happen and create wonderful things for myself. This has been the continuation of the healing process: loving myself enough to give myself joy and happiness.

Imagine that there are no limitations. Make a list of all that you desire and dream of. KNOW that it is there for you—Dream BIG! See yourself having all that you desire. Go for it!

Prepare for Lift Off!

One night I had a dream that a lot of people were on a gigantic airplane that was ready to take off. Suddenly an announcement came over the public address system to take our seats and that they were seating us with a dumb one next to a smart one. Everyone was laughing. I woke up laughing, realizing that we each wanted to believe that we were the smart one! Maybe the dream is true.

Imagine that you are the smart one in a situation or experience. You have greater tolerance, patience, and understanding for those with you. You were placed next to another person to help them.

Imagine that you are the dumb one in the situation. What is the person trying to teach you? What beautiful gift do they have to show you about yourself? Are you willing to learn from them? When you are truly loving, trusting, accepting, and approving of all people and situations, the divine energy within you flows freely out into the world, bringing light and joy, and returns to you tenfold and with its blessings! Knowing that there is nothing but God out there, you might as well relax and enjoy swimming in the ocean of love.

Saved By the Plow

I was doing a Reiki class in Grand Junction, Colorado, on Mother's Day. My contact and I decided to hold the class from 1:00 to 6:00 p.m., which would allow students to take Mom to breakfast as well as dinner. I had never seen that sort of scenery before and was captivated by the beauty. We decided to go up to the mesa before class. I didn't know what that was, but I really wanted to go. We grabbed a quick breakfast and took off. At that point, my contact wasn't so willing to go. I said, "I'm hearing, 'go for it.'" About an hour up the mountain, it started to snow.

The truck was swerving all over the road. On one side of the road was a wall of mountain, and the other side was a drop-off that seemed like it was a thousand feet down. I thought I should have listened to him, but when he said, "We can pull over and park," everything inside of me said quite emphatically, "I have to teach the second day of that class. We will be there!!!" All the power of the Universe was behind that intention, because within minutes a snow plow pulled up behind us. I think that it dropped from Heaven because we never heard it or saw it before it arrived. We let it go ahead of us and followed it all the way down the mountain. We arrived just a little late.

What I learned that day is that when you make a decision with all your heart and it is for the good of everyone, all of Heaven comes forth to help you. So set your intention and put all your energy and focus behind it, and you can achieve anything.

A Whale of a Tale

I went to the Dominican Republic to swim with the whales. I wanted to do this because the whales are said to be the record keepers, and I was hoping to receive some ancient wisdom from them. Swimming with these gentle giants of the sea was divine! My first experience with them was with a mama whale and her baby. We had to obey very strict rules.

We slipped quietly off the boat, and when we got near the whales, we had to hold hands and form a long chain to appear to be like a whale. We would then float above them while snorkeling and observe them. It was thrilling! We could see the milk as the baby was nursing. Mama stayed quiet beneath us, but the baby had to surface for air now and then. We were all touched by her trust of us with her baby. Even though the baby was as big as our boat, we still all felt honored. At one point I floated so close to Mom I was afraid I would touch her. That definitely was not allowed. After quite a long time, she made a powerful lurch and they were gone.

Another time we were in the boat watching a long chain of males head butt each other as they vied for attention from the females and for position in line to be the sperm donor. They were roaring like teenagers, powerful and noisy, while the females went on about their business. It was fascinating yet a bit scary, a show for us of nature in her power.

One night I was lying in my bed and asked the whales to share with me their wisdom. Suddenly a gigantic light came out of my solar plexus and I felt as though the whales shine out their light to bring light and love to the planet. It felt wonderful!

Later that night I opened *A Course in Miracles*. The lesson for that day was, "I Am the Light of the World." Talk about synchronicity. If we keep sending our light and love out to the world and blessing others, we can bring peace and create Heaven on Earth.

A student of mine told me a story that was told to her. It was so miraculous that I want to share it with everyone. She had recently met a man who was not even in the metaphysical community, which made his story even more wondrous. He had been in the Vietnam War, sharing a foxhole with five other men. Suddenly they were ambushed by the Viet Cong, who gunned down everyone around him. They even went back again and shot a buddy of his for the second time because they thought he had squirmed and was still alive. Meanwhile, this man just stood there waiting to be shot. They all walked away. No one had even seen him as he stood in the midst of them as though he were invisible. When he arrived home, his mother told him that she had blessed him every day and "saw him coming home safely." The beauty of this story reminds me of how much good we can do for one another. Be sure to send healing and blessings to all those in need. You can make a difference—in someone's life and in the world!

A Summary of Steps to Loving Yourself

Remember the dream. You were created in the image and likeness of God. You are as you were created to be. Give your life over to the God within you.

1. *Remember the Bowl of Truth.*
2. *Accept responsibility for all that you have created and know that you can change anything easily.*
3. *Love, nurture, and empower yourself by knowing that you are one with God. God is love. God is omniscient, omnipotent, and omnipresent. So are you. Look to the God within you for guidance and love. Feel the presence and the love within yourself.*
4. *Use affirmations, meditations, and visualizations to remind yourself who you really are and to create what you do want in your life. Remember the Huna principles—the world is what you think it is. Don't let it scare you!*
5. *Release all the limitation, anger, hatred, fear, anxiety, and anything else by using any or all of the exercises suggested throughout this book or any others that work for you.*

6. *Look in the mirror of your soul (other people) and see what others are showing you about yourself. Forgive yourself and others. Forgiveness releases the illusion of separation and changes your fears to love. Remember the message: If you're unwilling to forgive your brother/sister, you do not love God. Do the Forgiveness Exercise forever or until you love them and know that you are God. It brings miracles!*

7. *Send healing, light, and blessings to others as the whales do. It is magical and truly the gift of love. See others and yourself as the Holy Grail, holding the energy of the Divine.*

8. *Be grateful for your many blessings. Gratitude is an energy. It changes your attitude, and your life.*

Remember, to love another is to show them the beauty of his or her own soul. Do all of these with love in your heart. Prepare for joyous relationships and miracles to present themselves.

Love can't be far behind a grateful heart. —A Course in Miracles

A DIAMOND IS A LUMP OF COAL THAT MADE IT GOOD UNDER PRESSURE.
-Author unknown to me

Have fun. Enjoy the trip and the treasure that you are!

PEOPLE WHO DREAM
IMPOSSIBLE DREAMS
AND STRIVE TO ACHIEVE THEM
RAISE THE STATURE OF ALL
HUMANITY
A FRACTION OF AN INCH,
WHETHER THEY WIN OR LOSE
-Author unknown to me

THE PRESSURE IS ON
AND DIAMONDS ARE A
GIRL'S BEST FRIEND.
GO FOR IT!
-Nancy Retzlaff

Be a shining light unto the world and create Heaven on Earth.

About the Author

My life has been dedicated to God and the quest for healing and enlightenment. Wishing to overcome my trauma from childhood, I asked Spirit to help me and have received beautiful guidance every step of the way. I learned valuable techniques to change my fears to love, heal my body and mind, release addictions, calm the inner seas, bring light into the darkness, and manifest all that I desire. I would like to share these techniques with you. All of my books, stories, tapes, CDs, classes, and messages are designed to help you to transmute your own being, open to Spirituality, and create Heaven on Earth.

It all started with my parents' divorce when I was sixteen years old. War was raging all around me, and anxiety ruled the roost. In my fear I built a bomb shelter out of my body and hid deep inside. Consequently, I became nervous, neurotic and developed panic attacks. Eventually, the shelter, which was safe in the beginning, became a prison and I wanted out. All these delightful things going on in my body were the impetus to search for healing and happiness. I have been successful in overcoming all these difficulties and able to find love and joy

The beginning of my awakening was Concept Therapy, a class that states there is nothing but God and energy in the world and they are one and the same. The ideas that you hold establish the form for the energy to fill. Therefore, everything begins with an idea and consequently creates your reality. Then I found meditation, A Course in Miracles, a three volume book containing daily exercises to help you to become one with God, and Reiki, a laying on of hands healing modality. All of my studies and experiences have led me to greater avenues of awareness, love, truth, and fulfillment. I have learned so much from my experiences. I look forward to being able to bring these discoveries to you to enlighten your life and bring you Joy.

I was initiated as a Reiki Master on Babaji's ashram in Haidakhan, India in 1983 and have been blessed to teach Reiki all over the United States, in Hawaii, France, Israel, Thailand, and Japan. I was honored to be one of the first to re-introduce Reiki to the Japanese. I have been a teacher of Meditation and a Course in Miracles for thirty years, and am an ordained Minister of the Universal Spiritualist Association.

The services I offer are psychic readings, past life regressions, marriage and relationship counseling, in addition to spiritual counseling for weight loss and smoking cessation.

The initiations are all designed to open you to greater enlightenment. These include: "Awakening to Truth," a series of four attunements to bring forth the Love of God, the Light of God, the Power of God, and the Glory of God.